COMIC BOOK CULTURE
An Illustrated History

Ron Goulart

COLLECTORS PRESS

PORTLAND, OREGON

To Maggie Thompson, who mentioned my name.

Without the help of Jon Berk, attorney, collector, historian,
and Lou Fine idolater, this book would have 300 less illustrations.

A special thanks goes to Stuart Wells for his fine photography
of all these covers.

Copyright © 2000 Collectors Press, Inc.

For a free catalog write to:
Collectors Press, Inc.
P.O. Box 230986
Portland, Oregon 97281
Toll-free 1-800-423-1848

Principia Graphica *Design and Typography*
Ann Granning Bennett *Copy Editing*
Stuart Wells *Photography*

Distributed in Canada by McClelland & Stewart

Printed in Singapore

First American Edition

1 2 3 4 5 6 7 8 9

Library of Congress Cataloging-in-Publication Data

Goulart, Ron, 1933–
    Comic book culture : an illustrated history / by Ron Goulart. —
    1st American ed.
        p. cm.
    Includes bibliographical references.
    ISBN 1-888054-38-7
    1. Comic book covers—United States. I. Title.
NC1764.5.U6 G68 2000
741.5'0973—dc21

99-055708

Contents

INTRODUCTION

This is a book about pictures.

It isn't, however, about the sort of pictures that hang in art galleries and museums but rather about the pictures that once were found at the newsstand. In this case, the pictures appeared on the covers of comic books from the middle 1930s to the late 1940s ... the period usually referred to as the Golden Age of comic books.

And while this was definitely the first era of the superhero, not all the samples we selected show brightly costumed crimefighters battling evil and saving America from everything from rampaging robots to an invasion of hooded Nazis.

Sure, there'll be quite a bit of that sort of thing. But you'll also find a generous sampling of funny animals, funny humans, and some funny teenagers.

Magazine publishers had learned, as far back as the days of the fiction weeklies, dime novels, and the earliest pulp-fiction publications, that readers indeed judged a book by its cover. Comic book covers by the late 1930s served as provocative packaging for the product and as a potent advertising medium. Many of them equaled circus posters in terms of flamboyance, energy, and lettering. And sometimes what was promised outside wasn't exactly what was found inside.

There were simple comic book covers, complex covers, and some covers, admittedly, that didn't work at all. During the Golden Age thousands of covers came and went, competing for attention on the stands, eager to persuade customers to part with a dime. But in spite of the huckstering and mercenary motivations, illustrators created some very attractive covers. We've picked more than 400 of the best and preserved and organized them to illustrate a concise history of the birth and early growth of the comic book industry in this country.

Here you'll find some of the most effective output of admired artists such as Will Eisner, Jack Kirby, Lou Fine, Jack Cole, Alex Schomburg, and Bill Everett, plus many interesting but lesser known cartoonists like Paul Gustavson, Matt Baker, Gus Ricca, L.B. Cole, and Ramona Patenaude. Several of the covers have never been reproduced since their original appearance many decades ago.

While we offer an informative text outlining the birth and development of the modern comic book (and by modern we mean the format that's been around for roughly seventy years), *Comic Book Culture* is basically a picture book.

So take a look.

The story of comic books begins with newspaper comics. Long a part of America's newspapers, comic strips initially amused readers with slapstick humor and, mostly, simple and direct drawings. By the end of the 19th century, newspaper funnies were going strong, at least on Sundays. Comic books of various sizes and shapes, all of them reprinting newspaper strips, showed up soon after.

During the first decade of the 20th century an assortment of them arrived on newsstands. Among the earliest titles were *The Yellow Kid*, *The Katzenjammer Kids*, and *Buster Brown*. Comics featuring these characters were successful, but the strip most often seen in comic books during the years between the turn of the century and the advent of World War 1 was Carl Schultze's *Foxy Grandpa*. From 1901 to 1916 more than two dozen books reprinted his rather bland pages about a clever old duffer who continually outfoxed his two prankish nephews. "Bunny" Schultze's feature began in 1900 in the *New York Herald*, one of the newspapers involved in the earliest reprint publications. Their books, some of which were hardcovers, were colorful and ranged from twenty-four to fifty-two pages. Some measured as big as 10 by 15 inches, others were as small as 6 ½ by 7 ¼.

Nearly as popular as Foxy Grandpa was Buster Brown. The creation of Richard F. Outcault, Buster had the mind of a prankish Katzenjammer Kid inhabiting the body of a Little Lord Fauntleroy. Between 1903 and 1917, Buster appeared in nearly two dozen reprint comic books of various shapes, sizes, and colors. Winsor McCay's handsomely drawn *Little Nemo* made its appearance in just two comic books during these years. One was an 11 by 16 ½ inch color reprint of Sunday pages issued in 1906 and the other, 10 by 14, came forth in 1909.

The metropolitan newspapers themselves were among the earliest publishers of comic books. Late in 1902, William Randolph Hearst's *New York Journal* introduced five titles they described as "the best comic books that have ever been published." Each book had a cardboard cover, reprinted Sunday pages in full color, and sold for 50 cents. The titles, available from Hearst newspaper dealers across the nation, included Rudolph Dirks' *The Katzenjammer Kids* and F.B. Opper's *Happy Hooligan*. A book of Jimmy Swinnerton's kid strip *Jimmy* was released in 1905.

❶ •• *Bullets indicate relative value*
HAWKSHAW
1917
Unknown
The only comic book ever devoted exclusively to Gus Mager's Holmesian spoof.

❷ ••
BARNEY GOOGLE #1
1923
Billy DeBeck
A cardboard-covered, black-and-white reprint comic book from Cupples & Leon, with the strip's creator contributing an original cover and an introduction.

❸ ••
THE FUNNIES
August 30, 1930
Victor E. Pazmino
George Delacorte's first try at publishing comic books.

4 ·
Gulf Funny Weekly
1930s
Stan Schendel
A tab-sized
gas station giveaway.

5 ··
Comic Monthly #1
Polly & Her Pals
January 1923
Cliff Sterrett
Comic Monthly was the lone
forerunner to the ten-cent
comic books of the 1930s.

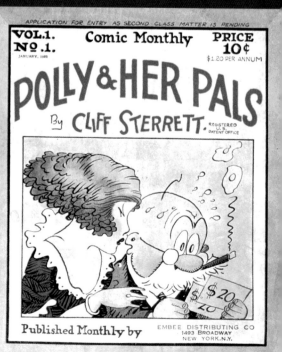

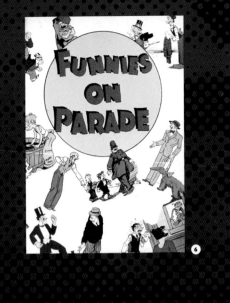

That same year the *Herald* reprinted McCay's *Little Sammy Sneeze*. The majority of the covers for these books were drawn by the strips' own artists, since the profession of cover artist, though well-established in the slick magazines and the burgeoning pulp-fiction titles, didn't exist for comic books.

Much of the color went out of comic books in the second decade of the century, when the black-and-white format became the standard. The daily comic strip, with Bud Fisher's pioneering *Mutt & Jeff* as the role model, was becoming increasingly popular. Ball Publishing, in collaboration with Fisher, published its first *Mutt and Jeff Cartoons* book in 1910. Selling for 50 cents, the book measured approximately 5 by 15 inches and reprinted one daily strip per page. In his joking preface, Fisher, one of the first cartoonists to benefit greatly from merchandising, admitted that the only excuse for publishing the book was "to get the money." Get it he did, since sales figures on that first book prompted Bell to publish four more books over the next six years.

The largest and most successful publisher of comic books during the first three decades of the century was the now nearly forgotten Cupples & Leon. Based in Manhattan, the firm published more than one hundred different issues of a variety of comic book titles between 1906 and 1934. They issued the majority of their output in the 1920s. Like most of its competitors in the then uncrowded field, Cupples & Leon reprinted newspaper comics and offered no original material. Among its titles were

Buster Brown, *Little Nemo*, *Mutt & Jeff*, *The Gumps*, *Bringing up Father*, *Smitty*, *Little Orphan Annie*, and *Reg'lar Fellers*. Toward the end of the company's involvement with the funnies, C&L reprinted three of the strips that became staples of the modern-format, full-color comic books of the 1930s—*Tailspin Tommy*, *Joe Palooka* and *Dick Tracy*. In 1934, after publishing final issues of *Little Orphan Annie* and *Bringing up Father*, the company took leave of comics to concentrate on its many boys'and girls' fiction titles.

Charlie Chaplin became a comic book character in 1917, when the M.A.Donohue Company of Chicago started a series of black-and-white books, reprinting the *Charlie Chaplin's Comic Capers* newspaper strip drawn by E.C. Segar, who went on to create Popeye. Clare Briggs' *Ain't It a Grand and Glorious Feeling?* panels were reprinted in 1922 and Harry Tuthill's *Home Sweet Home*, which later became *The Bungle Family*, appeared in 1925.

Edgar Rice Burroughs' famous jungle lord made both his comic strip and his comic book debut in 1929. The daily strip adaptation of *Tarzan of the Apes*, drawn by Hal Foster, started in newspapers in January. Later that year, Grosset & Dunlap issued *The Illustrated Tarzan Book*, which reprinted the first seventy-eight strips. While the cover of the 50-cent book said No. 1, there was never a second. When the book was reissued in the Depression year of 1934, the price was dropped to 25 cents. Mickey Mouse, cinema star since the late 1920s, first appeared in comic books in 1931. These, published by the David McKay Co. of Philadelphia, reprinted the *Mickey Mouse* newspaper

strips that were drawn by Floyd Gottfredson. The books appeared annually through 1934. Three of them offered dailies in black and white, the other Sunday pages in full color.

A pair of books that reprinted Segar's *Thimble Theatre* was published by the Sonnet Publishing Co. of Manhattan in 1931 and 1932. The books were priced at 25 cents and had cardboard covers much like those favored by Cupples & Leon. In 1935, McKay published two further books of Segar's opus, naming them after its by-then star Popeye. That same year McKay issued a comic book reprinting Carl Anderson's pantomime *Henry*. Both these strips were syndicated by Hearst's King Features. When King went into full-color, modern-format comic books in 1936, it was in partnership with McKay.

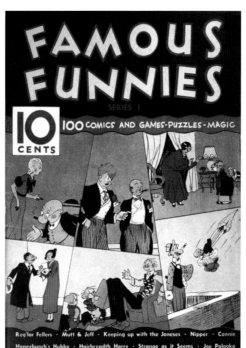

❶ ••••
FAMOUS FUNNIES
First Series 1934
Unknown
The result of someone at Eastern Color asking, "What would happen if we stuck a price tag on one of these and tried to sell it?"

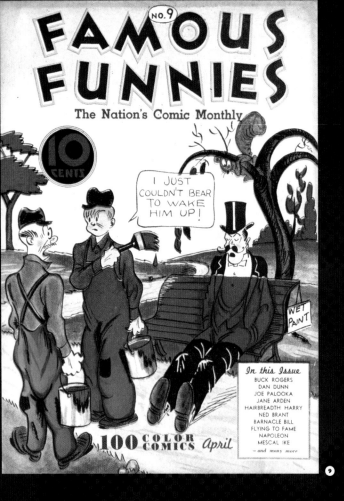

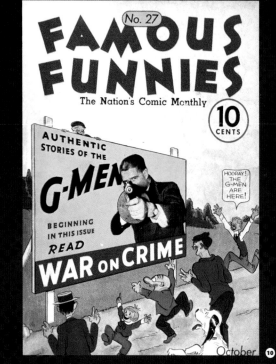

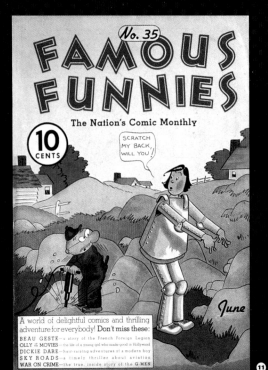

FAMOUS FUNNIES #9
April 1935
Victor E. Pazmino
Joe Palooka and the villain from *Hairbreadth Harry* join forces on the cover of an early issue of the new monthly.

FAMOUS FUNNIES #27
October 1936
Victor E. Pazmino
Turning to crime, *Famous* adds the G-Man comic strip *War On Crime* to its lineup.

FAMOUS FUNNIES #35
June 1937
Victor E. Pazmino
The Pazmino version of Ralph B. Fuller's *Oaky Doaks*.

FAMOUS FUNNIES #30
January 1937
Victor E. Pazmino
Another unlikely grouping of characters celebrating New Year's Eve.

FAMOUS FUNNIES #86
September 1941
Bill Everett
As the newsstand competition increased, *Famous* remodeled its covers and added action and danger.

In a sense, the type of comic books we've been considering so far are still with us. Books that reprint a popular newspaper strip in either paperback or hardcover have continued to thrive to this day. The best-selling trade paperback collections of *Dilbert*, *Garfield*, and *Calvin and Hobbes* are obvious examples.

About the only thing that came close to resembling a contemporary comic book in the years from 1900 to 1930 was an experimental magazine called *Comic Monthly*. It first hit the newsstands in January of 1922, with each issue devoted to a different comic strip. The magazine sold for a dime, gave the reader twenty-four pages with a black-and-white daily on each page and measured 8 ½ by 10 inches. It had a soft-paper cover and was distributed by the Embee Distributing Co. of New York City. The format owed a great deal to Cupples & Leon's two-bit comic books. But because of the 10-cent price, the cheaper paper, and, most importantly, the fact that it appeared on a regular monthly schedule, *Comic Monthly* was much closer to the comic books that emerged in the 1930s.

The first title in the twelve-issue series was Cliff Sterrett's *Polly & Her Pals*. Next came Rube Goldberg's *Mike & Ike*, followed by C.M. Payne's *S'Matter, Pop?* Subsequent reprints included *Barney Google*, *Little Jimmy*, *Tillie the Toiler* and *Toots & Casper*. The *Em* in the Embee company's name stood for cartoonist George McManus, creator of *Bringing Up Father*. His strip had been one of Cupples & Leon's best-selling titles since 1919, which probably accounts for the similar appearance of the two lines. The *bee* in Embee was

Rudolph Block, Jr. His father had joined the Hearst organization in 1896 and became the comics editor of the *Journal* and the *American*.

Early in 1929 George Delacorte, founder of the Dell Publishing Company, also tried his hand at inventing a comic book. What he actually produced, though, looked more like a tabloid funny-paper section. Delacorte had concluded that the best part of the Sunday newspaper was the comic section and therefore set out to produce one of his own. *The Funnies* was a twenty-four page tabloid with a third of its pages in color. A weekly, it sold for ten cents. In its pages could be found original features such as *Frosty Ayre* by Joe Archibald, *My Big Brudder* by Tack Knight, *Deadwood Gulch* by Boody Rogers and *Clancy the Cop* by Vic E. Pazmino, who usually signed himself VEP. Pazmino also provided most of the covers.

The Funnies struggled along for thirty-six issues before expiring. The editor of the brave but doomed venture was Harry Steeger, who went on to become a major publisher of pulp-fiction magazines in the 1930s and 1940s—*The Spider*, *Dime Detective*, *Black Mask*, *Adventure*, etc. But he never had anything to do with another comic book. Dell briefly tried the black-and-white format as well, adopting a Cupples & Leon style. In 1930, they issued VEP's *Clancy the Cop*. The following year came Rogers' *Deadwood Gulch*, plus a second *Clancy*.

The first regularly published comic book in the standard format was *Famous Funnies*. Though it got off to a shaky start and didn't climb out of the red until it had been in business for more than six months, it served as the cornerstone of what was to become one of the most lucrative branches of magazine publishing. For anyone who had a dime in the Depression year of 1934, *Famous Funnies* offered dozens of characters, all of them from the newspapers. The lineup included *Joe Palooka*, *Dixie Dugan*, *Hairbreadth Harry*, *Connie*, and the perennially popular *Mutt & Jeff*. *Buck Rogers* was added in the third issue. The covers, usually drawn by the ubiquitous VEP, showed gatherings of the various characters and promised "100 comics and games."

The inventor of *Famous Funnies* was Harry I. Wildenberg. He worked for the Eastern Color Printing Company of Waterbury, Connecticut. One of Eastern Color's specialties was printing the Sunday comic sections for several East Coast newspapers. Having an advertising background, Wildenberg first thought of using the comics as advertising premiums. He convinced Gulf Oil to give away a tabloid-size book of comics at its gas stations. The gimmick was successful, and Wildenberg continued to refine the idea. While contemplating extensions, he and some of his associates noticed that the reduced Sunday pages that they had made as a promotion for the *Philadelphia Ledger* would fit two to a sheet on a standard-size tabloid sheet of paper. Further fiddling and calculating enabled Wildenberg to work out a way to use Eastern's color presses to print sixty-four-page comic books.

The next problem was what to do with the printed and bound magazines. With the help of an Eastern salesman, Max. C. Gaines, Wildenberg first interested other advertisers in using comic books as premiums. Eastern produced books for Procter & Gamble, Canada Dry, Kinney Shoes, Wheatena, and other manufacturers of kid-oriented products. The give-away editions usually had print runs ranging from 100,000 to 250,000, but some went as high as one million copies.

Wildenberg and Gaines then considered sticking a 10-cent price tag on their comic books and selling them directly to children. The pair approached the Woolworth Five and Dime chain as a possible outlet but were informed that sixty-four pages of old comics didn't offer sufficient value for a dime. Eventually, in 1934, Wildenberg persuaded the American News Company to distribute a monthly comic book to

newsstands across the country. He called the new magazine *Famous Funnies*, a title he'd originally concocted for a soap-company premium. The initial issue sold ninety percent of its two hundred thousand copies. Although Eastern Color lost more than $4,000 on that one, by issue #12 *Famous* was netting $30,000 a month. Editorial offices for the fledgling magazine were set up in New York City. Harold A. Moore, a longtime Eastern Color employee, was listed as editor, but the actual working editor was Stephen A. Douglas. Brooklyn-born, Douglas had been working as a professional cartoonist before he even reached his teens. He was in his late twenties when he went to work as editor and production manager for *Famous*. During its early days, *Famous Funnies* reprinted mostly Sunday pages, including, besides those already mentioned, *Tailspin Tommy*, *The Bungle Family*, *Jane Arden* (complete with cut-out paper dolls), *Toonerville Folks*, and *The Nebbs*. As *Famous* moved into its third year, it began to make changes in its lineup. Several top Associated Press syndicated daily strips were added—*Scorchy Smith*, *Dickie Dare*, *Oaky Doaks*, and *Adventures of Patsy*. That meant the magazine was now offering artwork by some of the most gifted newspaper artists of the 1930s-men such as Noel Sickles, Milton Caniff, Ralph B. Fuller, Mel Graff, Coulton Waugh, and Bert Christman. It later added *Skyroads* by Russell Keaton and *Big Chief Wahoo* by Allen Saunders and Elmer Woggon. The sales of *Famous Funnies* climbed to a peak of more than 400,000 a month in 1939, but by 1941 because of enormously increased competition, they dropped to just a little over 250,000.

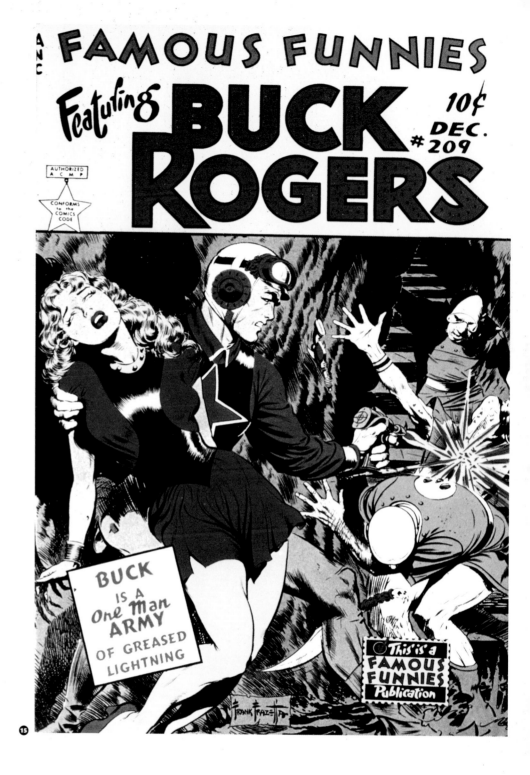

⓮ ··
FAMOUS FUNNIES #212
July 1954
Frank Frazetta
Buck Rogers was first seen
in issue #3 in 1934 and
remained until the last issue,
#218, in 1955.

⓯ ··
FAMOUS FUNNIES #209
December 1953
Frank Frazetta
Frank Frazetta contributed
a series of impressive
Buck Rogers covers for the
magazine's closing issues.

Jumping on the Bandwagon

eorge T. Delacorte founded Dell Publishing in 1921, using funds he'd parlayed from the one hundred dollars his father had given him when he graduated from college. His earliest magazines included pulps and true-confession magazines. He also published *Modern Screen*, the most popular movie magazine in America, *Inside Detective*, and *Ballyhoo*. Launched in 1931, this last magazine was an incredibly successful humor magazine put together by the inventive and irreverent Norman Anthony. *Ballyhoo* specialized in lampooning current advertising, and it soon reached a monthly circulation of two million copies. By 1934, it was bringing Dell profits of one million dollars yearly. Asked at the time if he intended the magazine as a force to reform advertising, Delacorte replied, "I wanted to make money."

Since he'd lost money with *The Funnies* back in 1929, Delacorte must have felt the times were better now in the mid-1930s for comic books. Being an organizer rather than a creator, he farmed out the production and printing of *Popular Comics*. Although the early statements of ownership list Dell of 149 Madison Avenue, New York City, as publisher and a gentleman named Arthur Lawson as editor, they don't tell the actual story of how *Popular Comics* was put together. It was packaged for Delacorte at the offices of the McClure Syndicate, whose color presses M.C.Gaines was using to cash in on the just commencing comic book boom. The presses, two of them, had been purchased from the defunct *New York Graphic*, Bernarr Macfadden's impressively sleazy daily tabloid newspaper. Gaines figured out to a way to rig the pair of two-color presses to print four-color comic books. He had been, as noted, present at the birth of *Famous Funnies*.

To edit *Popular* he hired Sheldon Mayer, a teenage cartoonist. "I went to work for M.C. Gaines in January of 1936," Mayer once recalled. "I had been up to see him the previous summer, and a half a year later he gave me a call and offered me a few days' pasteup work." That few days stretched into a few years and Mayer was eventually editing *Popular* and a string of subsequent magazines. He used both syndicate proofs and original art to make up his pages. The syndicates would be paid something like five dollars a page for reprint rights. Even though comic books were a hefty sixty-four pages at the time, this didn't require an enormous outlay of money.

The first issue of *Popular* was very much in the *Famous* mode, although the color was better and brighter and none of the copy was re-lettered to make it larger and more readable. Only Sunday pages were reprinted, and there was no new material except for the mandatory text story at the center of the book that postal regulations required. *Dick Tracy* led off the issue and strips from several rival syndicates were made use of, including *Skippy*, *Tailspin Tommy*, *Mutt & Jeff*, *The Gumps*, *Don Winslow*, *Little Orphan Annie*, *Smokey Stover*, *Believe It or Not*, and *Terry and the Pirates*. No attempt was

made to start the sequences at the beginning of a continuity. The better known features got four pages per month, the others just two.

By the time Mayer and Gaines ceased putting together *Popular*, somewhere near the end of 1938, it was running fewer reprints and had added a section of original material. All the Chicago Tribune-New York News Syndicate pages—*Terry*, *Dick Tracy*, *Annie*, etc.—had shifted over to the new *Super Comics* and had been replaced by mostly original features. One such was a series of six-page adaptations of Western B-movies, many the product of Monograph Pictures, and starring sagebrush stalwarts such as Tex Ritter, Gene Autry, and Jack Randall. *Popular* was now being printed by the Whitman division of the Western Printing & Lithography Company at its Poughkeepsie, New York, plant as part of a new agreement with Dell. Editorial work was done in the Manhattan office under the direction of Oskar Lebeck. A former stage designer and book illustrator, Lebeck served the magazine as artist, writer, and editor. He drew covers, wrote scripts, and initiated new features. Among them were *The Hurricane Kids*, *The Masked Pilot*, and *Gang Busters*. This last was adapted from Phillip H. Lord's highly rated weekly radio show.

The second monthly packaged by Gaines and Mayer for Dell was *The Funnies*. The first issue arrived on the stands late in the summer of 1936. Dell had already used the title for its unsuccessful original material tab, and the name was resurrected for the new reprint monthly. The early issues drew heavily

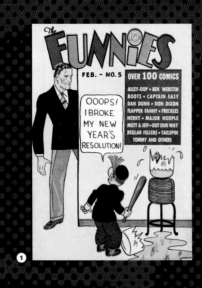

1 ··
The Funnies #5
February 1937
Unknown
A badly drawn early cover, whereon Dan Dunn interacts with one of the lads from *Freckles and his Friends*.

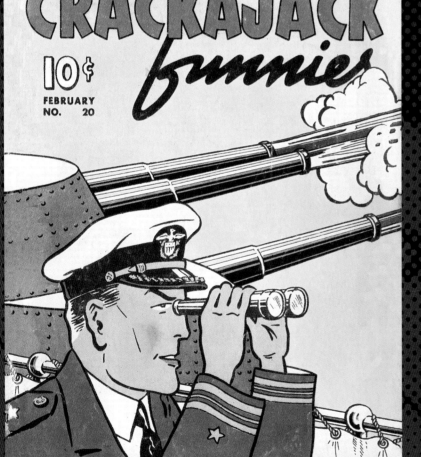

SUPER

MAGIC
MORRO

4 ••
SUPER COMICS #22
March 1940
Ken Ernst
By early 1940, many of the
reprint magazines felt the
need to add original heroes.

5 •
SUPER COMICS #33
February 1940
Richard M. Fletcher
Yet another original hero to
rub shoulders with Dick Tracy,
Smilin' Jack, and Terry.

DICK TRACY • SMILIN' JACK • TERRY and the PIRATES
LITTLE JOE • MAGIC MORRO • TINY TIM • HAROLD TEEN
and MANY OTHERS . . . All in full color

on the NEA syndicate stable, reprinting newspaper favorites such as *Alley Oop*, *Captain Easy*, *Boots*, *Out Our Way*, *Myra North*, and *Salesman Sam*. Among the other reprints were *Dan Dunn*, *Tailspin Tommy*, *Don Dixon*, and *Mutt & Jeff*. The latter, apparently one of Gaines' favorites, had also been in *Famous Funnies* and *Popular Comics*. In the second issue, editor Mayer, a boy cartoonist himself, at long last got to draw a feature. He introduced *Scribbly*, a strip about a boy cartoonist. The two or three pages per issue were laid out like Sunday pages, each with its own logo. Mayer did this so that his upstart creation could rub shoulders undetected with the real Sunday funnies being reprinted.

The third, and final, magazine the Mayer-Gaines team produced for Dell also had a simple direct title. *The Comics* made its debut with the March 1937 issue and, though billed as a monthly, took until March of 1939 to reach its eleventh, and last, issue. It was a hodgepodge of reprints, reruns, and original stuff. There were reprints of *Wash Tubbs*, and from the *Brooklyn Eagle*'s syndicate came *Bill and Davey*, a seagoing adventure done in cartoon style by James McCague, and *Gordon Fife*, a strip dealing with intrigue in mythical European kingdoms. From a sparsely distributed ready-print Sunday section turned out by the George Mathew Adams Syndicate came a cowboy strip *Ted Strong* by former Mexican caricaturist Al Carreno, along with a kid adventure titled *The Enchanted Stone* by Adolphe Barreaux and *Rod Rian of the Sky Police* by Paul Jepson. *The Comics* also made use of

5

Deadwood Gulch by Boody Rogers, *My Big Brudder* by Tack Knight, and *Clancy the Cop* by VEP. Delacorte was finally able to recycle some of the material from the original *The Funnies*.

In 1936, King Features Syndicate also entered the comic book business in partnership with the aforementioned David McKay Company. They produced a magazine titled, appropriately enough, *King Comics*. United Feature Syndicate, part of the Scripps-Howard empire, went Hearst one better and published its own magazines. The first of these was *Tip Top Comics*, which came forth in the early spring of that same year.

The earliest *Tip Top* covers were drawn by Mo Leff, a United staff artist, and depicted gatherings, usually improbable, of the magazine's various characters. On #1, for example, Tarzan and Li'l Abner are facing off in a boxing ring. Joe Jinks is the referee, and Mammy Yokum is her son's second. Among those to be seen ringside are Ella Cinders, Fritzi Ritz, and Hans and Fritz and the Captain. Inside readers found a potpourri of features, mostly reprinted, and greatly reduced, Sunday pages.

Some of the pages were several years old; others, like the *Li'l Abner* Sundays, were relatively fresh. There were three *Tarzan* pages per issue, originally from a handsome 1933 Hal Foster sequence dealing with a lost civilization run along the lines of ancient Egypt. Harry O'Neill's *Broncho Bill* and Leff's own boys' adventure fantasy, *Peter Pat*, provided the only serious

matter. The rest of the magazine was given over to humor, supplied by the likes of *Ella Cinders*, *Fritzi Ritz*, *Looey Dot Dope*, *Joe Jinks*, *Cynical Susie*, *Little Mary Mixup*, *Benny*, *Grin and Bear It*, and *The Captain and the Kids*. The first editor was Lev Gleason, who'd worked with Harry Wildenberg at Eastern Color. He went on to publish *Boy*, *Daredevil*, and *Crime Does Not Pay*, none of which were very much in the *Tip Top* style.

United's second monthly, *Comics on Parade*, was started early in 1938. The lineup was similar to what was to be found in *Tip Top Comics*, except that readers were given the daily versions of the strips rather than the Sundays. All of them appeared not in black and white but in glorious full color. After its twenty-ninth issue (August 1940), *Comics on Parade* underwent a format change. The rest of the issues were devoted to just one character per book. *Li'l Abner*, *The Captain and the Kids*, and *Nancy & Fritzi Ritz* alternated for several years, and then the frazzle-haired Nancy became the star of each issue until the title folded in 1955. *Sparkler Comics* was introduced by United in the summer of 1941. It was, more or less, the earlier *Comics on Parade* under a new title.

King Comics hit the stands at the same time as *Tip Top*. Both comic books were dated April 1938 and, by chance, both used the same basic cover idea, that of a prizefight. On *King*, you found Popeye walloping a gorilla while Jiggs refereed. The magazine offered a somewhat stronger lineup than its rival. On the adventure side, there were Sunday pages of *Flash*

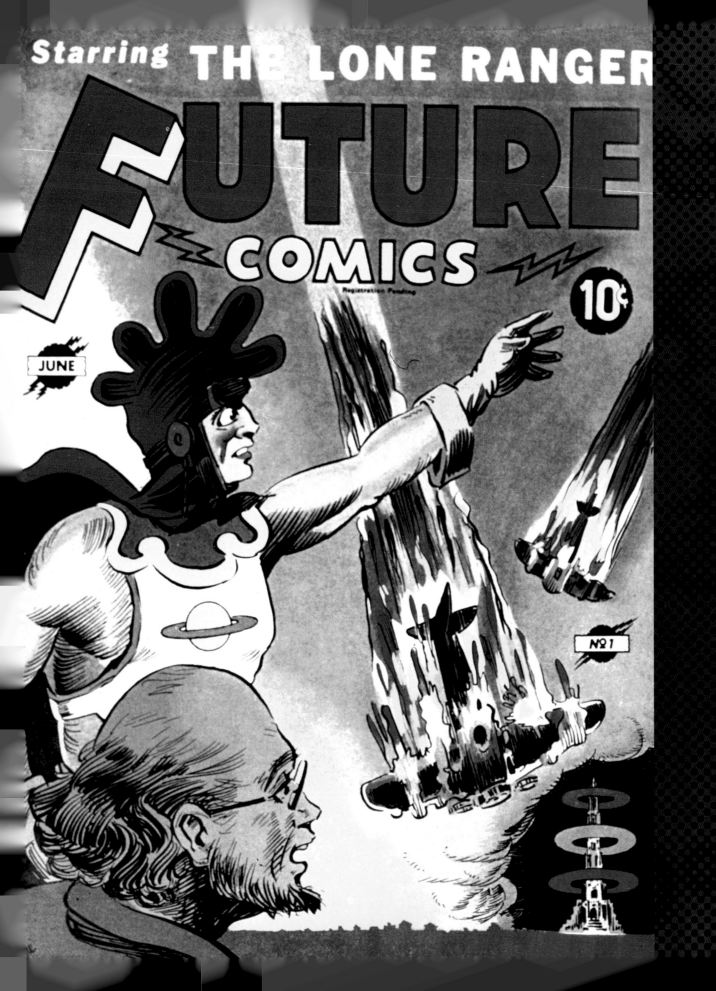

Gordon, complete with *Jungle Jim* topper, *King of the Royal Mounted*, *Mandrake* and *Tim Tyler's Luck*. Also crowded in were lesser known adventure strips such as *Curley Harper*, *Little Annie Rooney*, *Radio Patrol*, and *Ace Drummond*. Derring-do outweighed humor. Laughs were provided only by Popeye in Segar's *Thimble Theatre*, *Henry*, *Bringing Up Father*, and *The Little King*. Otto Soglow's red-coated monarch, who'd begun life a few years earlier in the pages of *The New Yorker*, also appeared in the magazine's cover logo.

Getting out *King Comics* was a joint effort that involved the Philadelphia editorial offices of McKay and the King bullpen in New York. Alexander McKay was the business manager and Ruth Plumly Thompson was the editor in Philly, while Joe Musial, Bud Sagendorf, and others handled the Manhattan end of things. The Philadelphia-born Miss Thompson is best remembered as the successor to L. Frank Baum. Chosen by Reilly & Lee in 1921, she wrote an Oz book a year until retiring as Royal Historian of Oz in 1939. For *King Comics* she also wrote poetry and filler text stories. The poems, which ran under the title *Sis Sez*, dealt with the misadventures of a freckled teenage girl and were illustrated by Marge Buell, who was the creator of *Little Lulu*. Marge also drew the pictures accompanying Thompson's fiction, which was in the Oz vein and featured characters such as King Kojo, Her Highness of Whyness, etc. The magazine later added *Barney Baxter*, *The Phantom*, and *The Lone Ranger*.

❽ ·
POPULAR COMICS #61
March 1941
Ralph Carlson
Before eventually returning
to comic-strip reprints,
the magazine even gave
superheroes a try.

Exactly one year after *King*, McKay started a second reprint title. It, too, was devoted to Hearst strips and was called *Ace Comics*. The emphasis was initially on the funny side. Early issues offered H.H. Knerr's version of the venerable *Katzenjammer Kids*, plus *Blondie*, *Pete the Tramp*, *Just Kids*, *Tillie the Toiler*, *Barney Google*, *The Pussycat Princess*, and *Krazy Kat*. For adventure fans, Ace used mostly heroes transferred from *King*, such as *Jungle Jim*, *Tim Tyler*, *Curley Harper*, and *The Phantom*. Later, Hal Foster's *Prince Valiant* was added.

Magic Comics appeared in the summer of 1939. The leading man, as the title hinted, was Mandrake the Magician. Besides offering *Mandrake* dailies by Lee Falk and artist Phil Davis, the early issues also included *Inspector Wade*, *Barney Baxter*, and *Secret Agent X-9*. In the humor department were such old standbys as *Blondie*, *Thimble Theatre*, and *Henry*. McKay's one attempt at a more flamboyant comic came along in June of 1940 and was a flop. Entitled *Future Comics*, it survived for only four issues and was an odd mixture of reprints and original material. Each issue offered several pages of *The Lone Ranger* plus a few of *The Phantom*. There were also two long original episodes of an adventure feature called *Rush Newton of the Newsreels* drawn by one time pulp illustrator Ralph Carlson.

The magazine's title was an allusion to the rather unusual science-fiction strip to be found within. Even so, *Saturn Against The Earth* was only given four pages. The strip was actually an Italian import. Known overseas as *Saturno Contro la Terra*, it was conceived by Cesare Zavattini (later to write screenplays with Fellini), written by Federico Pedrocchi, and drawn in impressively pulpy fashion by Giovanni Scolari. It first appeared in Italy at the end of 1937 and was offered as a Sunday page in the United States in 1940. After getting no takers, King stuck it into *Future*. Scolari later drew an Italian comic strip about Mussolini.

The first issue of Whitman's *Super Comics* had a cover date of May 1938. As mentioned, all its reprints were from the Chicago Tribune-New York News Syndicate roster. The stars of the new magazine were the dependable *Dick Tracy* and *Terry and the Pirates*, plus *Smilin' Jack*, *Little Orphan Annie*, *Moon Mullins*, and *The Gumps*. In the early years, it mostly consisted of dailies from as far back as 1935, reprinted with color added for the occasion. By the second year, Sunday pages only were being used. Since the continuity strips had stories that ran daily and Sunday, this practice resulted in some narrative gaps. The reprints were doled out in snippets of from two to four pages per issue. Oskar Lebeck was the first editor of *Super*. He also drew some of the original material filler pages himself.

The next month, with a cover date of June 1938, *Crackajack Funnies* was started by Whitman. Lebeck edited this one as well. The reprints relied heavily on what NEA had to offer, including *Wash Tubbs*, *Boots*, *Freckles*, *Out Our Way*, *Red Ryder*, and *Myra North*. From other syndicates came *Don Winslow*, *Dan Dunn*, and *Apple Mary*, which is what Mary Worth was calling herself in the 1930s. From the Saturday matinée screen came

Tom Mix and Buck Jones. Their adventures, laid out in imitation Sunday-page style, were reworkings of stories that had appeared in Whitman's fat, dime-store novels known as Big Little Books. These continued stories had titles such as *The Rock Creek Cattle War* and *Kidnappers of the Cholla Wash*. Art was by Jim Chambers, Jim Gary, and Ken Ernst. In each issue, Lebeck provided two or three pages of *Time Marches Back*—"The time machine is the famous invention of Looney Luke. With a simple twist of the dial it can transport him over the span of years into any age." *Stratosphere Jim* by Alden McWilliams began in #19 (January 1940). McWilliams wrote and drew this one, and it grew out of Lebeck's suggesting, "Why don't you do something with a super airplane?"

In *Crackajack* #23, Ellery Queen made his debut as a four-color sleuth. After a few months the artwork was taken over by Bill Ely. When interviewed years later, he couldn't recall who turned out the scripts but thought that Lebeck probably had a hand in the writing. Ely even suspected that he may have written a few of them himself. None of the twenty mysteries in *Crackajack* were based on the printed Queen canon, though one or two were adaptations of scripts used on the then-popular radio show. Frederic Dannay was not certain who did the comic book scripts either, but he was sure that he and Manfred Lee (who under the Ellery Queen pen name began collaborating on the writing the Queen novels and stories in 1929) didn't have anything to do with them.

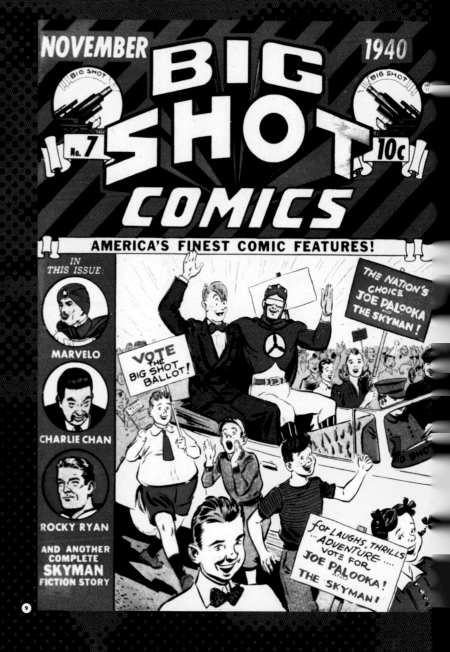

9 •

Big Shot Comics #7
November 1940
Creig Flessel
A successful mix of reprint strips—*Joe Palooka*, *Dixie Dugan*, *Charlie Chan*—and new material—*Skyman*, *The Face*, *Marvelo*.

10 ••

Feature Funnies #10
July 1938
Lank Leonard
Another early reprint book using the word funnies in its title.

Major Nicholson Enters the Fray

Major Malcolm Wheeler-Nicholson was a former U.S.Cavalry officer, a fairly successful writer of adventure yarns for the pulpwood fiction magazines, a first-rate raconteur and, above all, a gentleman. Dapper and well-groomed, he had an erect military bearing, carried a cane, and wore spats. Leaving the service in the early 1920s, he embarked on a career as a writer of fiction. He was soon selling to many of the most popular pulps, especially to *Adventure* and *Argosy*. His specialties were stories of military action around the world and historical tales of intrigue and swordplay. His was a name that editors would showcase on their covers.

Sometime in the autumn of 1934, the major, who was then in his middle forties, got a notion. He made copious notes, which he carried around Manhattan in an expensive-looking briefcase. After renting office space down on Fourth Street, Nicholson began recruiting artists and writers and seeking financing. What he had in mind was a line of comic books featuring nothing but original material. The company the major founded would eventually, under the name DC, earn countless millions. Nicholson, however, like many an innovator, went broke within a few years and never partook of those riches. Eventually, like many an old soldier, he just faded away.

His first magazine was called *New Fun*. What Major Nicholson had in mind was not exactly unprecedented. Dell, as noted earlier, had tried an original-material tabloid back in 1929. And the British had been doing somewhat similar comic papers for decades. Where Nicholson's magazine differed from what had been tried before in this country was the inclusion of adventure strips as well as funny stuff. *New Fun* offered the same sort of pulp-magazine and movie-derived action, intrigue and mystery that was becoming increasingly popular in the newspaper comic sections of the middle 1930s. The first issue had a cover date of February 1935. Touted as the "big comic magazine," it was a tabloid. While larger than *Famous Funnies*, it was nowhere nearly as colorful. The cover, which consisted of a cowboy page titled *Jack Woods* by Lyman Anderson, was in full color and bordered in bright red. But the thirty-two interior pages were black and white. All the new strips were laid out like Sunday funnies, and none, with a single exception, got more than one page.

Among the to-be-continued adventure features were *Sandra of the Secret Service*, *Jack Andrews, All-American Boy*, *Cap'n Erik*, *Buckskin Jim*, and *Barry O'Neill*. This last was in the Fu Manchu tradition, pitting pipe-smoking Barry against the insidious Oriental villain Fang Gow. Henry Kiefer, a European-trained illustrator, drew *Wing Brady*, about a flying Foreign Legion hero, and Adolphe Barreaux, who was also contributing the politely risqué *Sally the Sleuth* to the pulp *Spicy Detective*, produced his educational time-travel fantasy called *The Magic Crystal of History*. Clemens Gretter took care of science fiction, drawing both *Don Drake on the Planet Saro* and *2033/Super Police*. There was also an adaptation of *Ivanhoe* drawn by Charles Flanders in handsome Howard-Pyle style. Later, Flanders drew *Treasure Island* for the Major. This must originally have been intended for publication elsewhere, since each page ended by urging readers to "see next week." The humor features in *New Fun* included *Pelion and Ossa*, *Caveman Capers*, *Jigger and Ginger*, and Jack Warren's cowboy page starring Loco Luke. Tom McNamara, a newspaper veteran, drew *After School*, a kid page that was similar to the *Us Boys* strip he'd done for Hearst in the 1910s and 1920s.

Because of the shaky state of the Major's finances, he often didn't get around to paying his artists the small fees—usually five dollars per page—he'd promised them. Besides considerable ill will, this also produced considerable staff turnover. Lyman Anderson quit and was replaced by fellow pulp illustrator W.C. Brigham. Lawrence Lariar left, and Leo O'Mealia eventually inherited Barry O'Neill and Fang Gow; Barreaux gave way to Monroe Eisenberg. New artists and writers were also lured into the fold. Vincent Sullivan started doing a cartoony adventure page called *Spike Spalding* and Whitney Ellsworth contributed an *Orphan Annie* simulacrum named *Little Linda*. Contributions began coming in over the transom, too. From Cleveland came material from writer Jerry Siegel and his partner artist Joe Shuster. Their first feature to see print was *Doctor Occult*, which started in

New Fun #6 (October 1935). The youthful partners signed that with the pen names Leger and Reuths. The doctor was a ghost detective who "has sworn to combat supernatural evil in the world."

One of the reasons Major Nicholson was having money troubles was that his new magazine simply wasn't selling. The comic book boom had not yet begun when he first offered *New Fun* in 1935. Distributors were still reluctant to handle comic books, newsstands even more reluctant to give them rack space. Tom McNamara once recalled that the Fourth Street loft was usually piled high with unsold returned copies. By 1936, as noted earlier, *Popular*, *Tip Top*, *King*, and *The Funnies* would all be in business. The major was trying to gain a foothold with an over-sized magazine peopled by unheard of characters. A stubborn if not overly practical man, he was determined to hold on.

The Major and his editors, who were now Ellsworth and Sullivan, decided to utilize the venerable advertising practice of making your liabilities seem like assets and your differences like strengths. The lead page in the first standard-size issue—the magazine had been rechristened *More Fun*—explained that the magazine had changed because "so many people wrote in asking for *More Fun* in a smaller, handier size." It went on to extol the magazine's virtues. One was that "everything between the covers is BRAND NEW, never before published" and another was the fact that "all the pictures, type and lettering are clear and legible no eyestrain." *More Fun* now appeared much less like a compilation of rejected

MARCH, 1937

Detective COMICS

10¢

BRAND NEW!
ACTION-PACKED
STORIES IN
COLOR!

❸

newspaper Sunday pages. The straight stuff outweighed the humor, and just about every adventure feature ended with the words "to be continued."

Undaunted by the initial lack of success of his maiden magazine, the intrepid major had added a second title late in 1935. In shape, size, and look, the premiere issue was close to what was becoming the standard format for comic books, except that *New Comics* contained all of eighty pages, sixteen more than the usual amount, and had an uncoated, matte-finish cover. Like its predecessor, it offered a hodgepodge of adventure and comedy features, including *Castaway Island*, *Slim and Tex*, *Captain Quick*, *Dale Daring*, *Federal Men*, *Dickie Duck*, *Sagebrush n' Cactus*, and *J. Worthington Blimp, Esq.* Dubbed the "international picture story magazine," *New Comics* also couldn't afford color from cover to cover and some of the interior pages were printed in black and white. Included on the staff were John Mahon as business manager and William Cook as managing editor. Sullivan was initially assistant editor. Cook and Mahon soon defected to start a comic book of their own. With the sixth issue, *New Comics* dropped to sixty-four pages and with the seventh started using heavier stock for its covers. Work by Siegel and Shuster began appearing with #2 (January 1936). For this magazine they came up with *Federal Men*, starring grim, sharp-profiled Steve Carson of the G-Men.

The first Tarzan impersonator in comics burst forth in #5. This was Sandor by cartoon veteran Homer Fleming. "In the deep jungles of Northern India lives a strange white youth known as Sandor," explained the copy, "raised from infancy by a pack of wild dogs that now acknowledge him their leader." *Steve Conrad* was added with the fifth issue. Nicely drawn by illustrator Creig Flessel, the initial episodes were printed in black and white. Steve, described as "adventurer, scientist and inventor of the Cyanogen

Cruiser," was involved in exploring Dolorossa Isle, "a tropical island with mountain ranges, treacherous swamps, dense jungles and an abundance of vegetation it is not inhabited by man or beast!" This initial appraisal of real-estate conditions proved to be inaccurate, and soon Steve and his comrades, including a pretty blonde stowaway named Myra, were up to their elbows in murderous savages and their evil ruler. When color was added a few issues further along, readers learned that most of the natives of Dolorossa were bright green.

With the twelfth issue came a name change. *New* was transformed into *New Adventure*. Nicholson had decided that what readers wanted in an all-original comic book was less laughs and a lot more thrills. The covers became more serious and the interiors were overhauled as well. While almost all the adventure strips were still to be continued, they now covered from four to eight pages as opposed to a mere one or two.

Detective Comics got off to a modest start early in 1937. This was the final title to which the enterprising Major Nicholson attached his name. The first issue sported a bright crimson cover whereon a sinister Oriental was glowering at the reader. Vincent Sullivan served as editor and also drew the cover.

It was at about this time that Harry Donenfeld became more actively involved with Nicholson. An aggressive and gregarious man in his late thirties, Donenfeld had been active in several aspects of the magazine business for most of the decade. He published pulp magazines under several company

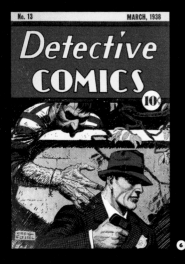

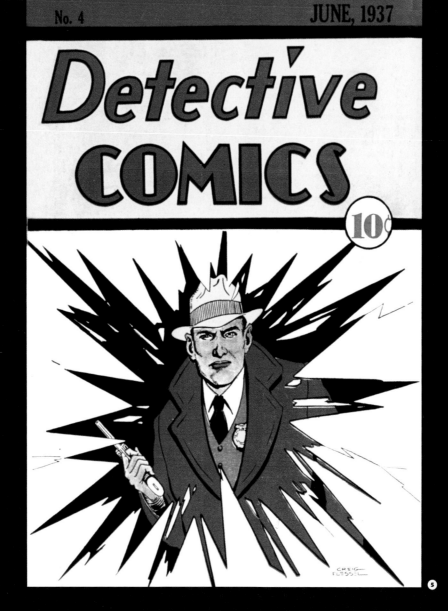

names—and even had a hand in the *Spicy* line—and was a partner in the Independent News Company distributing operation. He also operated the printing plant that ran the glossy covers for the Major's comic books. Nicholson, who owed money for those covers, had been advanced funds from Donenfeld's distributing wing. In order to get *Detective* going, Nicholson took Donenfeld as a partner. A new company was formed—Detective Comics, Inc.—and its owners were listed as Nicholson and J.S. Liebowitz. Liebowitz was Donenfeld's accountant. Nicholson remained with *Detective Comics* throughout its entire first year and then gave it up, along with his other titles, in 1938.

The new magazine contained, as the title promised, nothing but detectives. Over a half dozen of them plus humorous fillers dealing with mystery and sleuthing. Like the pulp magazines and the movies that inspired it, *Detective* offered action, suspense, and violence. Many of the stories also attempted formal mystery plotting, with an array of suspects and clues. There was a little bit of everything, from tough policeman to dapper amateur investigator. Speed Saunders was a plainclothes cop who covered the waterfront. The first artist on the feature was Creig Flessel. Major Nicholson himself wrote the adventures of Brad Nelson, a "crack amateur sleuth." An even suaver detective was Cosmo, also known as the Phantom of Disguise. For readers who liked a touch of the sagebrush in their mysteries, the magazine had Buck Marshall, who was a range detective.

Stuck at the tail end of *Detective* was Slam Bradley, an "ace freelance sleuth, fighter and adventurer." He was another creation of Siegel and Shuster.

Another of the early cover artists was Creig Flessel. He was there before the Golden Age officially arrived and he played an important part in the development of comic books, providing both stories and covers for some of the earliest original titles. A graduate of New York's Pratt Institute, he began doing illustrations in the middle 1930s for pulp-fiction magazines such as *The Shadow*, *Adventure* and *Crime Busters*. When Major Nicholson ran help-wanted ads in Manhattan newspapers, Flessel was one of those who responded.

More an illustrator than a cartoonist, Flessel specialized in adventure strips, which he drew and wrote. He quickly became Nicholson's star cover artist as well, replacing cartoonists such as editor Vincent Sullivan. For titles like *More Fun Comics*, *Adventure Comics*, and *Detective Comics*, Flessel initially had basically two sorts of illustrative covers. He drew cute kid stuff, which he later dubbed "warmed-over Norman Rockwell," and more dashing material that featured pirates, explorers, Foreign Legionnaires, deep-sea divers, and machine-gun-wielding gangsters. His covers served as provocative packages rather that as showcases for specific characters or situations to be found within. Because he was a gifted artist, Flessel's covers lent a definite touch of class to the Major's struggling list of titles. Later on, he also turned out several covers featuring *Adventure Comics*' newest masked man, The Sandman.

As noted, William Cook worked briefly in 1935 as managing editor on *New Fun*. In 1936, he and John Mahon, that other defector from Major Nicholson's camp, formed the Comics Magazine Company, Inc. Their first title was *The Comics Magazine* — within a few months it became *Funny Pages* — and it bore a May 1936 cover date on its first issue. Cook and Mahon promised their readers that everything was brand new and original and that "the creators of the features in this issue have established themselves with fans in all parts of the world." The early issues offered the same mixture of adventure and comedy as the Major's magazines. In fact, some of the strips were unpublished *New Fun* and *New Comics* material. Sheldon Mayer's *J. Worthington Blimp, Esq.* was there, Siegel and Shusters' Dr. Occult was practicing his ghost busting under the name Dr. Mystic, and *Federal Men* was altered and appeared as *Federal Agent*.

Later in 1936, *Funny Picture Stories* arrived, promising "Mystery, Thriller, Ace Adventure, Western" and introducing George Brenner's the Clock, the first mystery man in comic books. The Clock was a natty fellow who did his detecting in tuxedo and grey fedora. He covered his face with a black silken mask and carried a gold-headed cane. Brenner, who wrote and drew the feature, was no doubt influenced by Leslie Charertis' Saint as well as dapper pulp-crime fighters such as

the Phantom Detective. Just as the Saint left behind a card adorned with a haloed stick figure, the Clock left a card with the depiction of a timepiece and the slogan *The Clock Has Struck*.

The next offering from Comics Magazine Company was *Detective Picture Stories* and was devoted to the single theme of crime detection. Had Major Nicholson not been slowed by money problems, his *Detective Comics* would have beaten Cook-Mahon to the stands. Their subscription ad promised, "Here is a magazine crammed full of color, action, plot and punch. You'll see why crime does not pay, why the police always put the finger on the criminal." The stories were longer than those in the Nicholson magazines, up to ten pages, and all were self-contained. There were no regularly featured star detectives, and the story titles were reminiscent of those in pulp magazines—"*Murder in the Blue Room*," "*The Diamond Dick*," "*The Phantom Killer*," etc. Among the artists were Bert Christman, Ed Moore, and George Brenner. Although the first issue's cover promised a Clock story, none showed up inside. The fourth issue contained "Muss 'em Up," an early effort by writer-artist Will Eisner.

Despite a line of three titles, Cook and Mahon did not thrive. By the middle of 1937, they had sold out to an outfit called Ultem Publications. Ultem in turn sold its interests the following year to Joseph Hardie, who made the magazines the basis of his Centaur Publications, Inc. *Detective Picture Stories* became *Keen Detective Funnies* in the summer of 1938. Lloyd Jacquet, another Nicholson alum, acted as editor. The retitled magazine's first leading character was the Clock. Of the sleuths, a character with one foot in the costumed-adventurer camp was the Masked Marvel. Most of *Keen*'s other detectives were more prosaic and included Thurston Hunt, Terry Taylor, and Rocky Baird. In the sixth issue, a scientific investigator named Dean Denton joined the lineup. Over time, a variety of detectives continued to check in and out. There were Stormy Dawson, TNT Todd of the FBI, and Little Dynamite. The ubiquitous VEP drew Todd's adventures, and Little Dynamite was the first adventure feature by Jack Cole. Cole would go on to do exceptional comic book work in the 1940s.

A farsighted entrepreneur named Harry "A" Chesler was one of the first to suspect that there was going to be a comic book industry in America. His initial, by the way, didn't stand for anything and was stuck into the middle of his name and set off by quotes for no other reason than that Chesler fancied the way it looked. In 1936, Harry "A," who neither drew nor wrote, opened an office at 276 Fifth Avenue in Manhattan and set up what was the first comic art shop. Hiring artists and writers who'd work cheaply, he began to produce features for the original-material comic magazines. The field being what it was at the time, his shop had only two customers, Major Nicholson and the renegade Cook-Mahon outfit.

Late in 1936, Chesler made up his mind to do some publishing himself, and the result was two new titles, *Star Comics* and *Star Ranger*, both cover-dated February 1937. These were slightly larger than their newsstand competition, measuring 8 by 11 inches, but ran to just forty-eight pages.

Star Comics offered a blend of adventure and humor features, most of them of one to three pages in length. The exceptions were *Dan Hastings*, which took up eight pages, and *The Mad Goddess*, coming in at seven. The *Hastings* opus was laid out in Sunday-page style and bore a 1935 copyright date, indicating that Chesler had made an earlier unsuccessful attempt to peddle it as a newspaper feature. A science-fiction adventure, *Dan Hastings* was first drawn by Clemens Gretter and then carried on by Fred Guardineer. *The Mad Goddess* was set "in the jungles of South America" and drawn by Robert L. Golden. It was billed as "a complete adventure story." Other artists in the first issue were Creig Flessel, Fred Schwab, Henry C. Kiefer, and Dick Moores, who was represented by *King Kole's Court*, yet another unsold Sunday page. Moores eventually drew the *Gasoline Alley* newspaper strip.

Star Ranger, chock full of nothing but cowboys, both serious and whimsical, was one of the two original comic books devoted entirely to the West. Ken Fitch served as editor and wrote many of the stories. Several prolific pulp writers, including Norman Daniels and Tom Curry, also got credits. Among the early artists were Flessel, Guardineer, Schwab, and

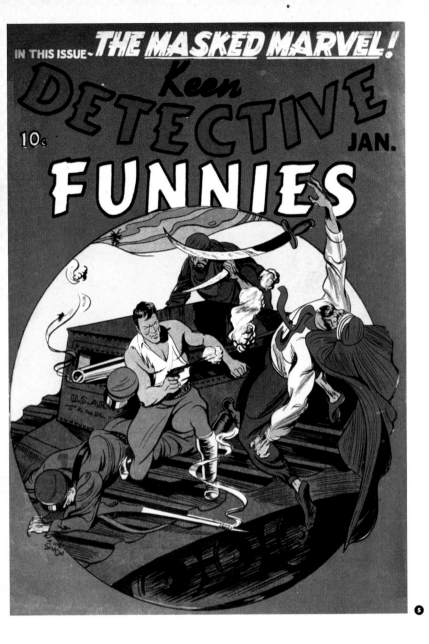

Rafael Astarita. After publishing half a dozen issues of each of the magazines, Chesler sold them. Eventually they came under Joseph Hardie's Centaur banner. *Star Comics* continued to concentrate on short material, an average issue containing as many as three dozen separate features. Among the contributors were artists Jack Cole, Ken Ernst, Bob Wood, and Charles Biro. Robert Winsor McKay, signing himself Winsor McCay, Jr., revived his father's best-known creation and drew some sadly uninspired *Little Nemo* pages for the magazine. In its later issues, *Star* included Tarpé

6 ••

DETECTIVE PICTURE STORIES #1
December 1936
William Allison
The first issue of the first all-detective comic book sported a pulp-style cover.

7 ••

DETECTIVE PICTURE STORIES #5
April 1937
George E. Brenner
Starring in yet another magazine, The Clock demonstrated his cracksman abilities.

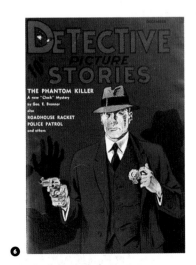

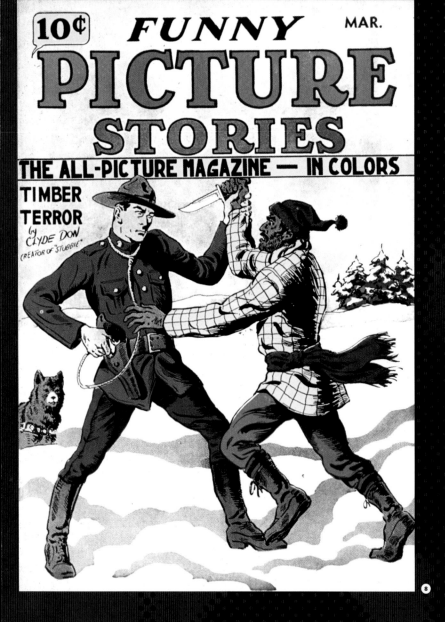

8

Funny Picture Stories #5
March 1937
William Allison
The Royal Canadian
Mounties were popular media
heroes in the 1930s. This one
is, hopefully, in the process
of getting his man.

Funny Pages v3 #1
February 1939
Fred Schwab
The Comics Magazine soon changed
its name. Most of its covers
aimed at being funny. The
prolific Schwab was still in his
teens when he drew this one.

10 ••

Funny Picture Stories #1
November 1936
George E. Brenner
The Clock was the very first
masked man created directly
for comic books. For his cover
debut, however, he doesn't
seem to be faring too well.

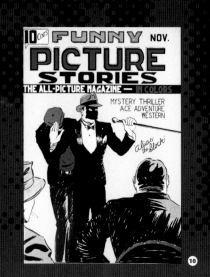

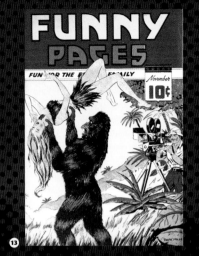

Mills' *Diana Dean in Hollywood*, Paul Gustavson's *Speed Silvers*, and Carl Burgos' *The Last Pirate*. All three of these artists went on to better things. *Star Comics* survived for twenty-three issues before expiring in the summer of 1939. *Star Rangers*, after undergoing a couple of title changes (*Cowboy Comics* and then *Star Ranger Funnies*), folded in the fall of the same year.

A few years earlier, in 1933 to be exact, three one-shot original detective comic books had made a limited appearance on a scattering of the nation's newsstands. They were thirty-six page black-and-white efforts with colored cardboard covers and measured roughly 10 by 13 inches. Norman Marsh, cartoonist and hustler, seems to have been the man behind publishing them. The titles were *Detective Dan*, *The Adventures of Ace King*, and *Bob Scully, the Two-Fisted Hick Detective*. Marsh, an aggressive former Marine, wrote and drew the one about Detective Dan, also known as Secret Operative No. 48. The other two were drawn by Martin Nadle, a cartoonist and puzzle maker who later worked for DC Comics, Inc. Ace King was also called "The American Sherlock Holmes."

While the magazines promised further issues, none ever appeared. At the end of his *Detective Dan*, Marsh assured readers that they'd find "In the next issue—Wu Fang King of the Dope Smugglers—Don't Miss It. More Thrilling Than Ever." A blatant *Dick Tracy* imitator, *Detective Dan* resurfaced in 1934 as the newspaper strip *Dan Dunn*. Under that name, as we've seen, he had a moderately successful career in early reprint comic books.

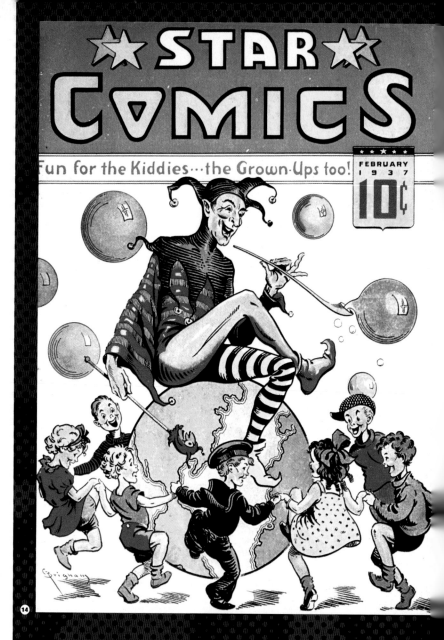

STAR COMICS #1
February 1937
W.C. Brigham
The early issues, published by Chesler, were filled with more than two dozen one-and two-page features, most of them intended to be funny.

STAR COMICS #5
July 1937
Robert McCay
Many years earlier, Robert McCay had been the inspiration for his father's *Little Nemo* newspaper page.

THE DAWN OF THE GOLDEN AGE

For several decades, the term Golden Age has been applied to comic books of the 1930s and 1940s by fans, collectors, dealers, and historians. It was initially used, years ago, in the fanzines put out by pioneering enthusiasts before the first comic conventions had even been held. There was never, however, any unanimous agreement as to exactly what year the Golden Age began and when it officially ceased. *Overstreet's Comic Book Price Guide* defines it as "the period beginning with Action #1 (June 1938) and ending with World War II in 1945." *The Comics Buyer's Guide*, though, says that the term "indicates the first era of comic book production—which occurred in the '30s and '40s."

For the purpose of our discussion, we'll define the Golden Age of Comic Books as running from the late 1930s, marked by the advent of Superman and his earliest imitators, through the deluge of costumed crimefighters and into the late 1940s, by which time the majority of superhumans had just faded away.

The initial superhero and quite probably the most important comic book character ever created was Superman. The invention of author Jerry Siegel and artist Joe Shuster, Superman single-handedly turned the fledgling comic book business into a major industry, forever changing the look and content of the four-color magazines. The thirteen-page story that introduced the Man of Steel in the first issue of *Action Comics* was mostly cobbled together from Siegel and Shuster's unsold Superman newspaper strip. It offered a one-page intro to the new hero, listing his birthplace only as "a distant planet" and making no mention of his real or adoptive parents. Page two began in the middle of the story, with the costumed Superman carrying a pretty nightclub singer through the air. It also managed to introduce the mild-mannered Clark Kent and his newspaper co-worker, Lois Lane, who was already giving him the cold shoulder.

By the fourth issue, sales of *Action Comics* had leaped forward. They quickly rose to five hundred thousand, and by 1941 the magazine was selling nine hundred thousand copies each month. The separate *Superman* magazine, begun in 1939, soon reached a circulation of 1,250,000 and grossed $950,000 in 1940. These impressive figures didn't go unnoticed by other publishers and editors, and by the time the 1940s started, a full-scale superhero boom was underway.

The boom was a mite slow to get going. For the rest of the year following the introduction of Superman, no further superhumans were introduced, not even by DC. *Action*, in fact, featured the Man of Steel on just three of its first dozen covers. Only two costumed crimebusters, neither of whom possessed a single superpower, entered comics. It wasn't until the spring of 1939 that a second true superhero came along, and he managed to remain on the job for just one month.

The earliest costumed hero to venture onto the newsstands after the Man of Steel was the Arrow, who could be found in *Funny Pages* #21 (September 1939) onward. He fought crime with a bow and arrow, wore a red costume with a roomy hood that completely hid his face. Paul Gustavson was the artist. The Crimson Avenger, who was modeled fairly closely on the successful Green Hornet of radio, was the only other dress-up crimebuster to come along in 1938. He commenced wielding his gas gun in *Detective Comics* a month after the Arrow first dipped into his quiver.

The first authentic superhero to set himself up in competition with Superman was Wonder Man, who appeared exactly once, in Victor Fox's *Wonder Comics* #1 (May 1939). Will Eisner provided story and art and much later observed that Fox had asked him for a character whose "specifications were almost identical to Superman." DC thought so, too, and sued, which caused Wonder Man to vanish after his maiden flight. But the enterprising Fox, a former accountant with DC, didn't give up his dream of cashing in on what he was certain would be a superhero bonanza. He would soon return to try again.

Detective Comics #27 appeared at just about the same time as the first issue of *Wonder*, containing DC's next entry in the hero derby. There on the cover was a fellow called The Batman, swinging over the rooftops with an armlock around the throat of a hoodlum in a green pinstripe suit. Inside, the new hero led off the issue in a short, six-page story. Although the pointy

No. 7 **DECEMBER, 1938**

64 PAGES OF THRILLS!

Action Comics

10¢

Reg. U S Pat. Off.

SUPERMAN APPEARING IN THIS ISSUE AND IN EVERY ISSUE

3 •••

NEW YORK
WORLD'S FAIR COMICS #2
1940
Jack Burnley
The first time Superman,
Batman, and Robin were seen
in public together.

NEW YORK 15¢
WORLD'S FAIR COMICS
1940 ISSUE
96 THRILLING PAGES IN FULL COLOR!
SUPERMAN · BATMAN AND ROBIN
THE SANDMAN · SLAM BRADLEY

3

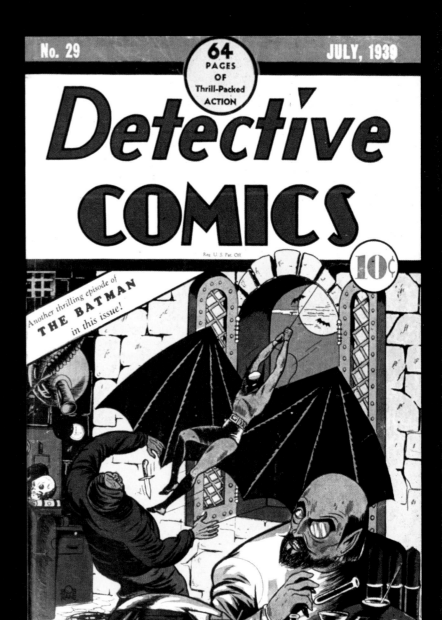

No. 29 JULY, 1939

64 PAGES OF Thrill-Packed ACTION

Detective Comics

Reg. U.S. Pat. Off.

10¢

Another thrilling episode of THE BATMAN in this issue!

1 •••

Action Comics #1
December 1938
Joe Shuster
The Man of Steel's second
appearance on a cover.
This is the actual copy of
Action Comics that was used as part
of the evidence in the lawsuit
brought against upstart
superhero Wonder Man and his
upstart publisher Victor Fox.

2 ••••

Detective Comics #29
July 1939
Bob Kane
The second cover
showcasing The Batman.

Funny Pages #34 (v4 #1)
January 1940
Harold DeLay
The Arrow had a nifty costume, an unfailing knack for sensing upcoming crimes and great skill with a bow and arrow, but no super powers at all.

5 ··
Fantoman #4
December 1940
Lew Glanz
"The one and only Fantoman" was actually the Fantom of the Fair. A change of name and a change of venue didn't help, and he was soon out of business.

Wonder Comics #1
May 1939
Will Eisner
The first Superman impersonator in what turned out to be both his debut and his farewell appearance.

8 ··
Amazing Mystery Funnies #16
November 1939
Paul Gustavson
Like several of his contemporary costumed heroes, the Fantom preferred using his fists rather than weapons.

6 ··
Amazing Adventure Funnies #1
June 1940
William E. Rowland
Although an unsuccessful character, the Fantom managed to appear in several titles.

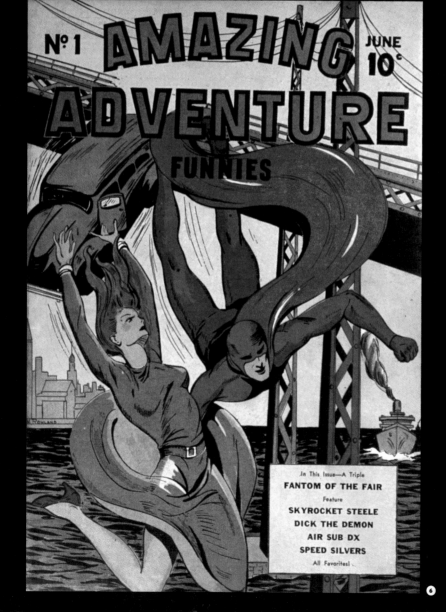

ears on his cowl were a little lopsided and his batwing cape didn't fit exactly right, there was something intriguing about him. For a costumed hero without one single magic power, he has managed to survive quite well while hundreds of latter-day competitors have fallen by the wayside. Bob Kane was the artist, Bill Finger the writer. The following year, soon after Jerry Robinson joined the team as Kane's assistant, Batman acquired a youthful sidekick in the person of Robin the Boy Wonder.

In 1939, America held two world's fairs. One was in San Francisco and one in New York, and that same year the Fantom of the Fair was born—"a new super thrilling strip! Packed with exciting action which takes place in a world's fair." The adventures of the dark-clad, hooded hero were drawn by Paul Gustavson. The Fantom, with some changes and modifications in his outfit as time went by, was to be found in Centaur's *Amazing Mystery Funnies* from the eleventh issue (July 1939) through the twenty-fourth (September 1940).

In the summer of 1939, the unsinkable Victor Fox came back for another try. He introduced not one but three new costumed heroes. The #3 issue of *Wonderworld*, his revised title for *Wonder*, introduced the Flame. The initial adventures of the yellow-clad superman were handsomely rendered by Lou Fine. A slow starter, the Flame took several issues to get his act together. Finally, he started living up to his name and revealed a hitherto unsuspected knack for bursting into flame, burning through walls, etc. In *Wonderworld* #30 (October 1941), the Flame made

another addition to his mode of operation by taking on a female companion. Known as Flame Girl, she stuck with him until the magazine folded after three more issues.

Fox's second magazine was *Mystery Men Comics*, and in that one he offered two costumed heroes. The intended leading man was the Green Mask, who wore a costume and cape of blue and green and a green head-rag mask. The first artist was Walter Frehm. The Blue Beetle started out toward the back of the book, appearing in short, four-page adventures. Eventually he started showing up for work in the distinctive blue chain-mail outfit and domino mask that became his trademark. An artist calling himself Charles Nicholas was responsible for the earliest escapades of the Beetle. As captions continually pointed out, the Blue Beetle came by his powers by ingesting something known as Vitamin 2X. In everyday life, he was a uni-formed cop named Dan Garrett. When he grew impatient with the law's delays, he popped into his favorite pharmacy for a dose of 2X.

Among the other early superguys were Amazing Man, an early invention of Bill Everett, who debuted in Centaur's *Amazing Man Comics* in the autumn of 1939; Shock Gibson, a Human Dynamo in a red cos-tume and odd yellow helmet, who began life in *Speed Comics* #1 (October 1939); Doll Man, the diminutive do-gooder invented by Will Eisner and Lou Fine, who started in *Feature Comics* near the end of 1939; Samson, a long-haired muscleman who was born in Fox's *Fantastic Comics*.

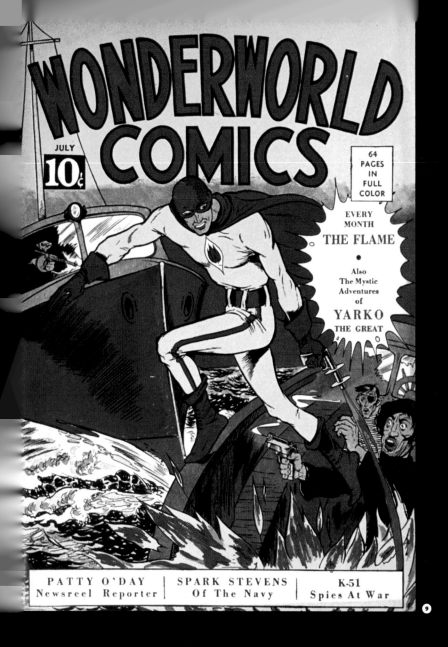

9

9 •••

Wonderworld Comics #3
July 1939
Lou Fine
The unsinkable Victor Fox
was back. *Wonder* had a new title
and a brand-new superhero,
The Flame. The Eisner-Iger
shop provided the character and
the artist, the gifted Lou Fine.

10 ••

Wonderworld #7
November 1939
Lou Fine
Skeletons and near skeletons
were popular on early covers.

11 ••

Wonderworld #28
August 1941
Edd Ashe
The answer to the cover
question about "What manner
of monster was this?" was never
answered inside the magazine.

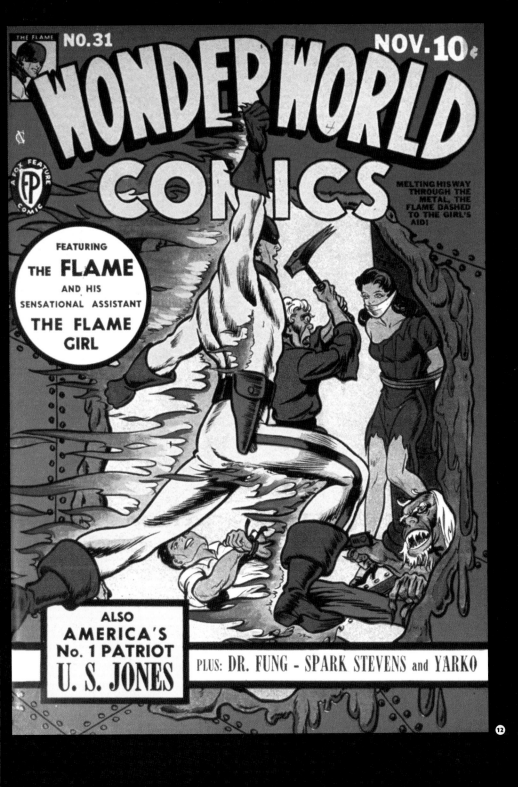

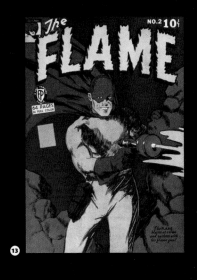

⑬ ••
THE FLAME #2
Fall 1940
Edd Ashe
The Flame soon had a separate book of his own. Here he's shown using his flame gun.

⑭ ••
THE FLAME #8
January 1942
Pierce Rice and Louis Cazeneuve
Late in 1941, the Victor Fox comics empire suffered a temporary collapse, and all his titles ended. The Flame was not rekindled until the 1950s.

⑬

⑫ ••
WONDERWORLD #31
November 1941
Pierce Rice and Louis Cazeneuve
Although the Flame's new assistant, Flame Girl, was mentioned in the cover copy, she was never shown. That's an entirely different girl he's in the process of rescuing.

15 • •

MYSTERY MEN COMICS #1

August 1939

Lou Fine

Most of the Fox cover heroes started out as gun enthusiasts. Here the Green Mask, another new character, is blasting his way into the lair of a mad doctor.

16 • •

MYSTERY MEN COMICS #3

October 1939

Lou Fine

The ultimate fate of the blonde young woman remained a mystery, since this was another cover that had nothing to do with any story to be found within.

15

16

17

17 • •

MYSTERY MEN COMICS #8

March 1940

Lou Fine

The Blue Beetle uses his gun to blast some villains with a fondness for morbid tattoos.

18 • •

REX DEXTER OF MARS #1

Fall 1940

Dick Briefer

A regular character in *Mystery Men*, Rex appeared in just one issue of his own title. The Kooba touted in the cover copy was a soft drink Victor Fox was promoting.

The first issue had a somewhat muddy painted cover by pulp old-timer Frank R. Paul and was called just plain *Marvel Comics* (November 1939). Veteran pulp-magazine publisher Martin Goodman was calling his company Timely Publications at that point. Funnies, Inc., another early freelance shop, run by Lloyd Jacquet, that was packaging comic books, pro-

duced the new magazine's lineup of characters. These included durable characters such as the Human Torch, Sub-Mariner, the Angel, and Ka-Zar. With the second issue, the title was expanded to *Marvel Mystery Comics*. Eventually Goodman's entire company would change its name to Marvel.

What Carl Burgos, the artist-creator of the Human Torch, had stumbled on was a basic idea that had tremendous appeal to the young boys of the day. Most of them went through a phase where they were touched with a little pyromania—they played with matches, yearned after fireworks, attempted to concoct fiery explosives with their chemistry sets. With the Human Torch, they had a hero who could play with fire and get away with it. The notion was strong enough that Burgos' admittedly less than masterful drawing couldn't smother it.

Beyond a doubt, contributing to the early success of *Marvel* were the battles and team-ups of the Torch and the Sub-Mariner. Bill Everett's Prince Namor had been raising hell from the very first issue. Coming to Manhattan from his decimated undersea kingdom, the Sub-Mariner was determined to seek revenge. "You white devils have persecuted and tormented my people for years," he explained to pretty policewoman Betty Dean, with whom he had a long-running love-hate relationship. Once he arrived in New York City, Namor behaved in the manner of an earlier and larger visitor named King Kong. With the angry prince cutting up in the Big Apple and the Human Torch freshly arrived to work as a cop, a confrontation was inevitable.

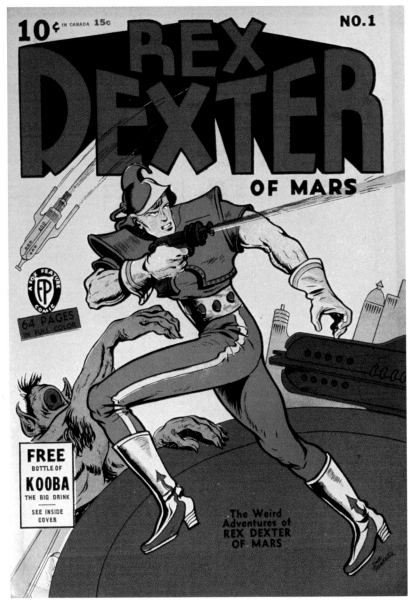

What followed was a battle royal that raged through *Marvel* #8 and #9 and wound up in a standoff in #10. "Something New! Human Torch Battles the Sub-Mariner," proclaimed the copy on the cover of #8. And the next issue, which showed the Sub-Mariner tearing down the supports for an elevated train, sported even more excited copy—"22 Thrill-Packed Pages! The City Was Rapidly Being Wrecked As The Sub-Mariner Ran Wild. Could The Human Torch Stop This Mad Destruction? Read This Amazing Battle of The Super-Humans!" The intricate and detailed cover was an early example of the work of the commendable Alex Schomburg. By #17 (March 1941), as America moved closer to war, the two feuding super-humans called a truce and teamed up—"26 Smashing Pages of Human Torch and Sub-Mariner Fighting Side By Side!" Another Schomburg cover, showed the duo trying to thwart "gigantic plans for an invasion of the United States!"

Timely's second title was *Daring Mystery Comics*, and it came along late in 1939. Not destined for success, the magazine tried a variety of characters including the Texas Kid, Monako—Prince of Magic, the Fiery Mask, Marvel Boy, Carl Burgos' the Thunderer, and Bill Everett's other aquatic hero, the Fin. *Mystic Comics* came next and also was not a hit. It tried heroes such as Blue Blaze, Flexo the Rubber Man, the Black Marvel, Super Slave, and the Blazing Skull. Next was added the Destroyer, an avenger operating in Europe who had "sworn not to rest until he had destroyed the Nazi hordes." An early scriptwriter was Stan Lee.

DC went more enthusiastically into the super-hero business in 1940, when *More Fun* #52 (February 1940) introduced the Spectre. Written by Superman's Jerry Siegel and drawn by Bernard Baily, it starred murdered cop Jim Corrigan who came back as the Spectre to fight crime in ghostly form. The magazine added another weird hero a few months later. Dr. Fate was the invention of writer Gardner Fox and was drawn in a stylized spooky fashion by Howard Sherman. "Dwelling apart from mankind in his lonely tower north of ghost-ridden Salem is the mysterious Dr. Fate," explained an early caption, "who calls upon secret and ancient sources for the power with which he fights unusual crimes." Fate wore a blue and gold costume and a metal helmet that completely covered his face. He specialized in beating ancient Mayan gods, combating globemen from outer space, defeating horrors from the cosmic void, and counseling young women who feared they might be wereleopards. A fan of H.P. Lovecraft and *Weird Tales*, Fox's early yarns were among the oddest super-hero stories of the era. The Spectre appeared on the majority of covers from #52 through #67. Then Dr. Fate showed up on the next nine, replaced by the Green Arrow and Speedy, who did a bow-and-arrow version of Batman and Robin.

The first true superhero to grace the pages of *Adventure Comics* was Bernard Baily's Hour-Man, introduced in #48 (March 1940). A caption explained that a young scientist named Red "Tick-Tock" Tyler had recently discovered "Miraclo, a powerful chemical that transforms him from a meek, mild scientist to the underworld's most formidable foe with Miraclo he has for one hour the power of chained lightning-speed. But unless he performs his deeds of strength and daring within one hour, the effects of Miraclo wear off and the Hour-Man becomes his former meek self." *Adventure*'s next superhero was auspiciously launched in #61, getting the cover and the lead-off position. Starman was yet another laconic and mild-mannered playboy who moonlighted as a crime fighter. He flew by holding tight to his gravity rod. Artwork was by Jack Burnley, with the majority of scripts by Gardner Fox.

The character destined to unseat all the magazine's hopeful heroes had been around for awhile, but no one had been paying much attention to him of late. Then in #69 of *Adventure Comics* (December 1941),

the Sandman got a new look—an updated costume complete with yellow tunic and tights, purple cowl, cape and boots, and a boy companion named Sandy. Chad Grothkopf wrought these changes and left after one issue, followed by two more by Paul Norris. Next came the team of Joe Simon and Jack Kirby, and they turned the venerable avenger into a hit. Kirby's exuberant pencilling and stories that had the heroes confronting dreams and nightmares as well as colorful villains won a large audience for the revitalized hero and he and his boy sidekick were showcased on every cover from #74 to #102, a run of nearly four years.

19 ••
WEIRD #9
December 1940
Edd Ashe
Ever since Robin had joined up with Batman a few months earlier, boy wonder sidekicks had become a fad. The Dart had a young fellow named Ace as his partner from his first story onward.

20 ••
MYSTIC COMICS #2
April 1940
Alex Schomburg
Dynamic Man bursts into a set-up that looks like it was designed by Rube Goldberg. This sort of complexity became a Schomburg specialty.

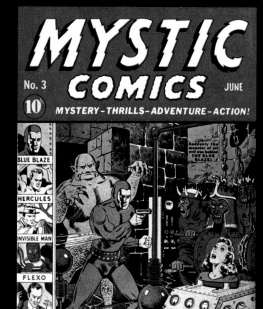

21 ··
Mystic Comics #6
October 1940
Alex Schomburg
The Destroyer was battling
Nazis long before the United
States entered the War.

22 ··
Mystic Comics #3
June 1940
Alex Schomburg
Looking quite a bit like the
Blue Beetle, Blue Blaze comes
to the rescue.

Late in 1938, M.C. Gaines entered into an agreement to produce a series of comic books that would be published under the DC umbrella. The initial titles, edited by the still youthful Sheldon Mayer, were *Movie Comics* and *All-American Comics*. Both appeared with cover dates of April 1939. The short-lived *Movie Comics* offered adaptations of current movies, using very badly reproduced stills with the dialogue balloons' captions lettered in. Mayer loathed the magazine and later claimed they were forced to do it.

While *All-American* featured some original material, it contained not a single superhero at the offset and relied on newspaper strip reprints to fill many of its pages. Of the many characters shown on the bright yellow cover of the first issue, only Mayer's Scribbly was an original, and the blurb announced—"The only comic monthly with all your old favorites: Mutt & Jeff, Ben Webster, Tippie, Reg'lar Fellers, Skippy." Mayer later said that Gaines, despite being instrumental in the emergence of Superman, didn't think the kid public would be interested in any further costumed heroes.

About the closest thing to a superhero was Ultra-Man, a futuristic adventure character who commenced in #8 (November 1939). Set in the United States of North America in the year 2239 and starring a heroic fellow in red tunic, green shorts, and eagle-crested helmet, the feature was a creation of Jon L. Blummer, who was also doing the boy-aviator strip, *Hop Harrigan*, for the magazine. Succumbing to superhero fever in the summer of 1940, *All-American* introduced the Green Lantern in its sixteenth issue. There he was on the cover, decked out in his red-green costume and charging along a girder at a machine gun-wielding thug. That cover was by Sheldon Moldoff. The eight-page origin story was by writer Bill Finger and artist Mart Nodell. Irwin Hasen, who worked in a loose cartoon-style version of the Milton Caniff style, ghosted most of the Lantern stories from #26 through #51 (July 1943) and drew the story in #27 that introduced the Green Lantern's unorthodox sidekick, the pudgy cabdriver Doiby Dickles. Hasen was also responsible for more than two dozen covers. Once *All-American* opened its doors to the Green Lantern, other costumed crime fighters and superheroes began moving in. The Atom, Dr. Midnite, and Sargon the Sorcerer soon followed.

By the time Gaines and Mayer got around to planning their next title late in 1939, things were changing. The youths who bought comic books were quite obviously willing to support more than one superhero. So when *Flash Comics* #1 (January 1940) appeared, it contained two superheroes plus a masked avenger. The star was the Flash, "the man who moves with the speed of light." Harry Lampert was the original artist, soon followed by E.E. Hibbard. The Hawkman was first drawn by Dennis Neville and then, for a good part of its run, by Sheldon Moldoff. Rounding out the early crew were The Whip, a Zorro impersonator; Cliff Cornwall, a daredevil secret agent; and Johnny Thunder, a nitwit who was looked

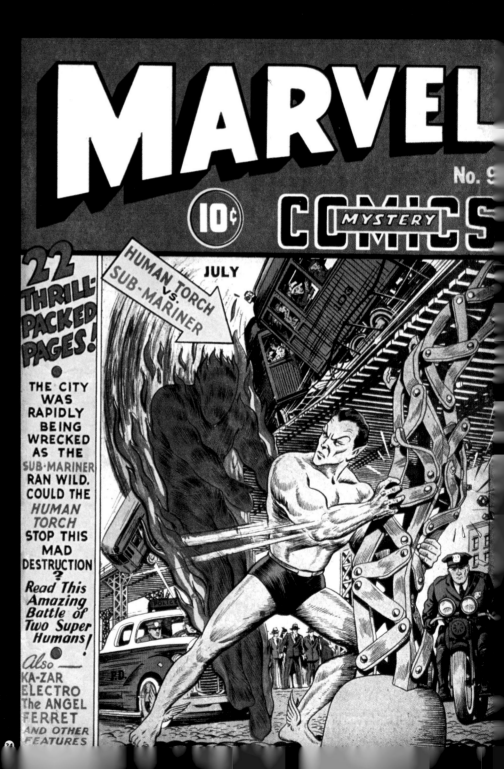

Marvel Mystery Comics #5
March 1940
Alex Schomburg
The Human Torch's first cover appearance in his perfected form.

Marvel Mystery Comics #9
July 1940
Alex Schomburg
The second round in the "Amazing Battle of Super Humans."

Motion Picture Funnies Weekly #1
April 1939
Fred Schwab
Packaged by the Funnies, Inc., shop and intended as a theater giveaway, it only made it through one issue. The Sub-Mariner was first seen in its pages.

ALL-WINNERS COMICS #1
Summer 1941
Alex Schomburg
A couple of losers also got
into the magazine.

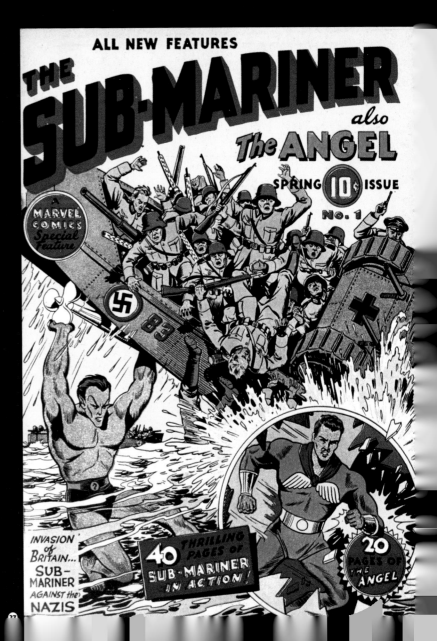

26 • • • •
HUMAN TORCH #2
Fall 1940
Alex Schomburg
Despite the number, this was
the first issue of the Torch's
own magazine.

27 • • • •
SUB-MARINER #1
Spring 1941
Alex Schomburg
The Sub-Mariner, looking
somewhat larger than life in
this instance, was also an early
battler of the Nazis.

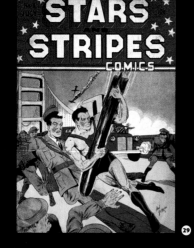

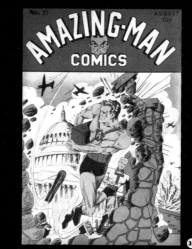

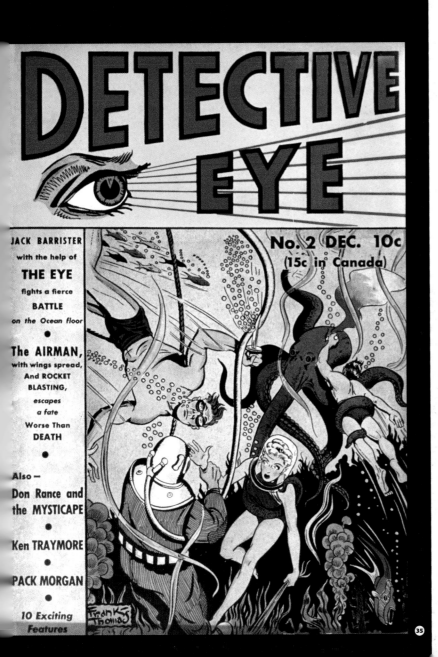

ALL-FLASH #7
November-December 1942
Louis Ferstadt
The "Fastest Man Alive"
soon branched out from *Flash
Comics* into a book of his own.
The incomparable Ferstadt
often drew in a style that
showed touches of a distinct
Cubist influence.

after by a somewhat snide thunderbolt. Newspaper veteran Ed Wheelan drew *Flash Picture Novelets*, which eventually became *Minute Movies*, a comic book version of his once-popular comic strip.

The final monthly from the Mayer-Gaines combine was *Sensation Comics*. The first issue bore a January 1942 cover date and showcased Wonder Woman, who had been introduced in *All Star Comics* #8 shortly before. A somewhat bizarre feature in its early days, one that went in for bondage as much as for crime fighting, it was the creation of psychologist William Moulton Marston and venerable cartoonist H.G. Peter. The rest of the *Sensation* cast included Mr. Terrific, the Gay Ghost, Little Boy Blue, and Wildcat. Drawn by Irwin Hasen and written by Bill Finger, *Wildcat* dealt with a boxing champ who donned an animal skin to fight crime.

One of Sheldon Mayer's most enduring inventions was *All Star Comics*. Begun as a quarterly, it brought together characters from various DC monthly titles. Issue #3 (Winter 1940) saw the first meeting of the Justice Society of America—with Sandman, the Atom, the Spectre, the Flash, Hawkman, Dr. Fate, the Green Lantern, and Hour-Man attending. From then, on the JSA teamed up in each issue to defend the country against spies, travel to the far planets, feed the starving peoples of Europe, and defeat such super villains as the Brain Wave, the Psycho-Pirate, and Degaton. All the novel-length adventures were written by the inventive and prolific Gardener Fox, with the heroes' regular artists usually drawing individual chapters.

38

ADVENTURE COMICS #75

June 1942

Joe Simon and Jack Kirby

The new, improved Sandman and his boy wonder sidekick, Sandy, confront Jack Kirby's earliest version of Thor.

39

MORE FUN COMICS #54

April 1940

Bernard Baily

The mystical Spectre often shot up to gigantic proportions.

Bill Everett, Lou Fine, Ramona Patenaude

Bill Everett. Both a high-school and art-school dropout, William Blake Everett had been on the art staffs of newspapers in both Boston and New York before entering, while in his early twenties, the comic book field in 1938. A writer as well as an artist, his earliest work was for the Centaur line where he created characters such as Skyrocket Steele, Dirk the Demon, and Amazing-Man. He later joined with Lloyd Jacquet, his former editor at Centaur, and became art director at Jacquet's Funnies, Inc., shop. They provided art and editorial content for comic books such as *Blue Bolt*, *Target Comics*, and *Marvel Mystery Comics*. It was for *Marvel* that Everett created his most successful and long-lasting character, the Sub-Mariner.

Among the many other characters he drew over the years were water-based ones such as The Fin, Hydroman, and Namora. He also drew the Patriot, Sub-Zero, The Chameleon, Marvel Boy, and Marvel's Daredevil. Although he never got to draw his Sub-Mariner on a Golden Age cover, Everett provided quite a few covers for the Centaur line and later for titles such as *Blue Bolt*, *Heroic Comics*, and *Famous Funnies*. He died in 1973.

1 ··

AMAZING MYSTERY FUNNIES #3
November 1938
Bill Everett

One of Everett's earliest
covers, poster-like in its
simplicity of design and color.

2 ··

AMAZING MYSTERY FUNNIES #9
May 1939
Bill Everett

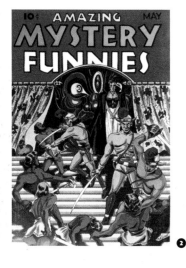

3 ··

AMAZING MYSTERY FUNNIES #6
February 1939
Bill Everett

4 ·

BLUE BOLT #14 (V2 #2)
July 1941
Bill Everett

5 ··

BLUE BOLT #11 (V1 #11)
April 1941
Bill Everett

Dick Cole was the creation of
Everett's friend, and Funnies,
Inc., colleague, Bob Davis.

6

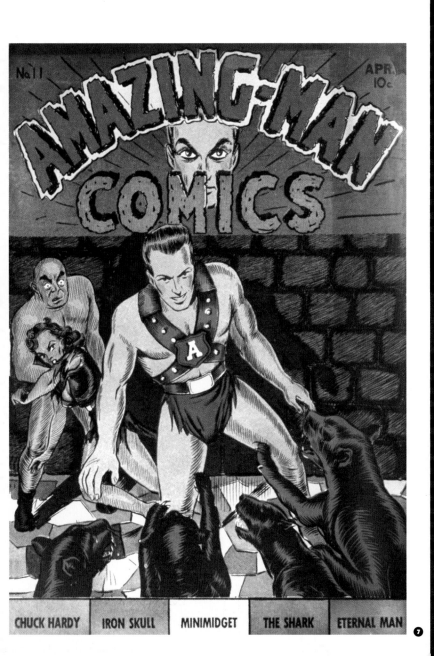

7

One more of Everett's
aquatic heroes.

VICTORY COMICS #1
August 1941
Bill Everett

A few months before Pearl
Harbor, the Funnies, Inc.,
gang produced this new title,
which offered "10 New Smashing
War-Action Features."

Lou Fine. A gifted and influential artist—often referred to as "an artist's artist"—Fine's career in comic books lasted only a few years, from the late 1930s until the middle 1940s. A New York boy, Louis Kenneth Fine studied at the Grand Central Art School and Pratt Institute. Partially crippled by childhood polio, he yearned to be an illustrator, and among his major influences were Dean Cornwell, J.C. Leyendecker, and Heinrich Kley. He went to work for the Eisner-Iger shop in 1938 and soon was drawing for the Fiction House and Fox lines on such features such as *Wilton of the West*, *The Count of Monte Cristo*, and *The Flame*. Later, he worked directly for Quality, drawing *The Black Condor* and *The Ray*. From early on, Fine's specialty was covers, and he turned out dozens of them. He worked then in an exuberant, heroic illustrational style and possessed a strong sense of design and color. Like many good packages, his covers were usually much more interesting than what was to be found within.

By the middle 1940s, after a spell of ghosting Eisner's *The Spirit*, he moved into drawing Sunday advertising strips for the funnies. His accounts included Pepsi-Cola, Postum, and RKO Radio Pictures. He next drew two moderately successful newspaper strips, *Adam Ames*, a soap-opera effort, and *Peter Scratch*, about a tough private eye who lived with his mother. Fine, who'd long since abandoned his flamboyant comic book style, died in 1971.

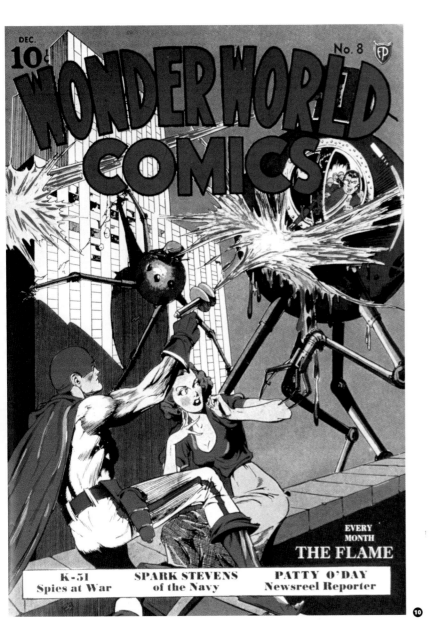

WONDERWORLD COMICS

⑩ ••

WONDERWORLD COMICS #8
December 1939
Lou Fine
An exceptional young artist,
Lou Fine was only in his
middle twenties when he drew
the following selection of
impressive covers.

⑪ ••

WONDERWORLD COMICS #4
August 1939
Lou Fine

⑫ ••

WONDERWORLD COMICS #11
March 1940
Lou Fine

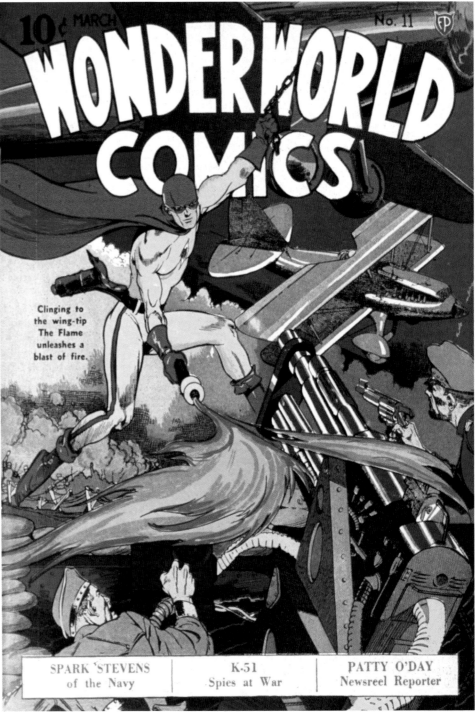

Fantastic Comics #1

December 1939

Lou Fine

Stardust • Space Smith • Sub Saunders • Capt. Kidd

❶❹

❶❸ •••

Fantastic Comics #3

February 1940

Lou Fine

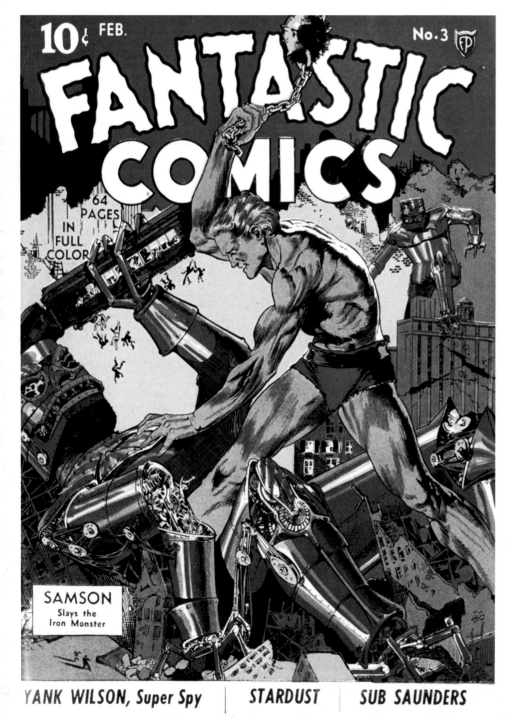

SAMSON
Slays the
Iron Monster

YANK WILSON, *Super Spy* | *STARDUST* | *SUB SAUNDERS*

❶❸

❶❺ ••

Jungle Comics #1

January 1940

Lou Fine

Kaanga was the earliest of the
Tarzan impersonators in
comic books.

❶❺

THE EAGLE · COSMIC CARSON · PERISPHERE PAYNE **16**

THE EAGLE · DR. DOOM · PANTHER WOMAN **17**

18

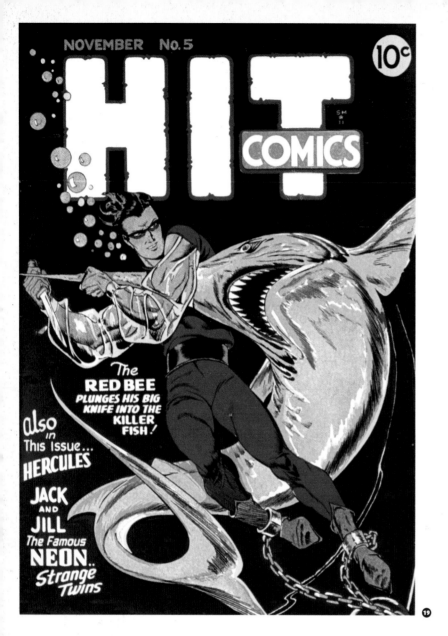

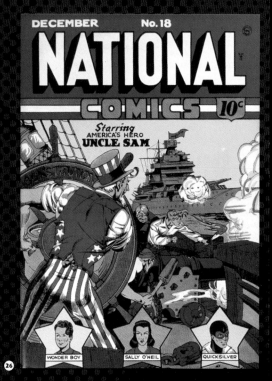

26

The Uncle Sam story in this issue, on the stands sometime in November of 1941, included an enemy attack on Pearl Harbor.

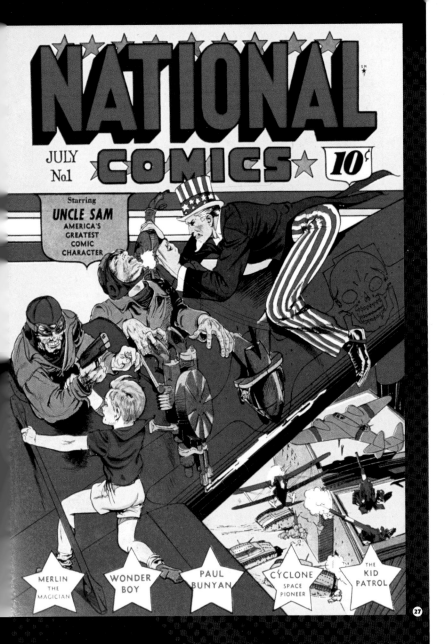

Ramone Patenaude. She remains a mystery woman, and little is known about her. She surfaced in the early 1940s, first at MLJ and then at Fox, Marvel, and Novelty. For most of her brief career, she worked out of the Funnies, Inc., shop, and the only name she ever signed to any of her work was "Pat." For the inside of comic books she drew characters such as the Green Falcon (a knight, not a superhero), V-Man, Dynamo, Dr. Fung, and The Vision. For Fox she drew an impressive and bold series of covers; for Novelty's *Target Comics* she produced a few milder and quieter ones. She left the field in 1946, one of the few women cartoonists to draw covers during the Golden Age.

27 •••
NATIONAL COMICS #1
July 1940
Lou Fine

28 ••
NATIONAL COMICS #11
May 1941
Lou Fine

29 ••
TARGET COMICS #28 (V3 #4)
June 1942
Ramona Patenaude
One of her more sedate covers.

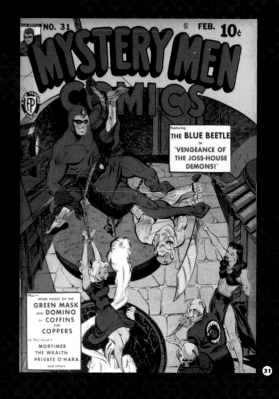

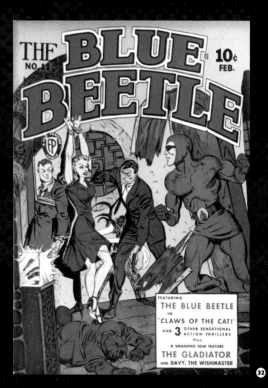

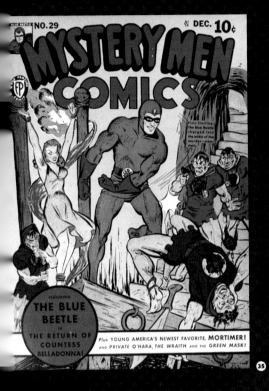

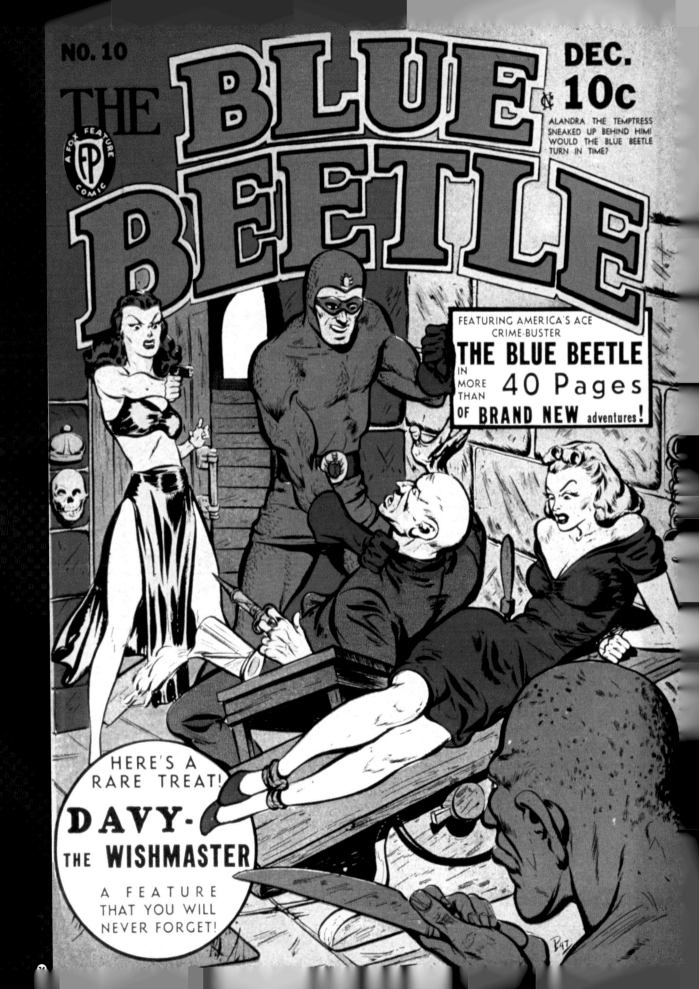

The most popular and best-selling superhero of the 1940s turned out to be not Superman but rather a red-clad upstart who never took his profession completely seriously. Created by artist C.C. Beck and editor-writer Bill Parker, Captain Marvel was introduced in the first issue of Fawcett's *Whiz Comics* early in 1940 and within a few years he was outselling not only Superman but also every other costumed crimefighter who'd followed in the Man of Steel's wake.

Toward the end of 1939, Fawcett Publications, Inc.—producers of magazines such as *Captain Billy's Whiz-Bang*, *True Confessions*, *Mechanix Illustrated*, and *Motion Picture*— sent out a promotion piece to magazine distributors across the country. The mailer announced the company's entry into the comic book business and the imminent publication of *Whiz Comics*, which would star Captain Marvel, "another character sensation in the comic field!" Fawcett promised wholesalers a comic book that was "here to stay." Their forthcoming title would lead the parade and bring "permanent profits." This was, ultimately, a rare instance of advertising hyperbole coming absolutely true.

Parker had come up with a variation of the dual-identity theme. Despite the fact that Captain Marvel was the World's Mightiest Mortal, he was really a young teenager named Billy Batson who needed the magic word "Shazam" to turn into a

❶ •••••
WHIZ COMICS #2
February 1940
C.C. Beck
Like Superman, Captain
Marvel was seen tossing an
automobile around on his
initial cover appearance.

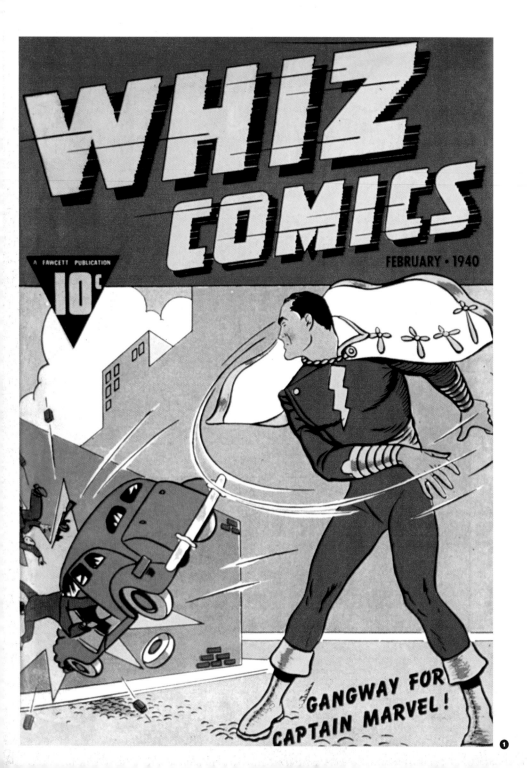

superman. It was always to his own identity that Billy returned when the trouble had passed. The subsequent adventures had a tremendous appeal to kids. They concerned a boy who was able to take a shortcut to adulthood whenever a serious problem came up. Billy became, in a way, his own tough and protective big brother or ideal father. The adventures also had a great visual appeal, primarily due to Beck, who'd been working for Fawcett as a staff cartoonist since the middle 1930s. His Captain Marvel stories exemplified his philosophy of drawing, being models of simplicity, clarity, and design. They were fun to look at as well as read. Beck also drew the majority of the hundred and fifty some *Whiz Comics* covers. He based the Captain's looks on those of Fred MacMurray, one of the most successful of the comedic leading men of the movies in the late 1930s and early 1940s. The costume, particularly in its earliest phases, was adapted from that of a typical light-opera soldier.

Whiz Comics also housed characters such as the magician, Ibis the Invincible; the Western hero, the Golden Arrow; the seafaring Lance O'Casey; and the scourge of saboteurs, Spy Smasher. As the demand for more Captain Marvel stories increased—in addition to *Whiz*, the Captain began appearing in *Captain Marvel Adventures* and *America's Greatest* in the early 1940s—Fawcett first went to outsiders and then had Beck set up a shop of his own. Among the outsiders were Joe Simon and Jack Kirby, who produced a rather sketchy first issue of *Captain Marvel Adventures.* Beck's first assistant was a one-time pulp illustrator

2 •••
FLASH COMICS #1
January 1940
C.C. Beck
The ashcan edition—a black-
and-white demo put together for
copyright purposes—of what
became *Whiz Comics*. At this point,
the world's Mightiest Mortal was
named Captain Thunder.

3 ••
CAPTAIN MARVEL ADVENTURES #7
February 6, 1942
C.C. Beck

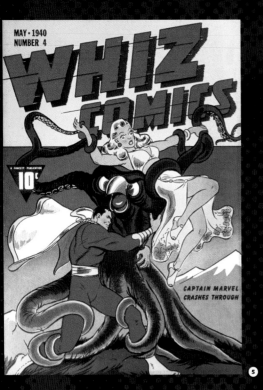

named Pete Costanza, and he later added Morris Weiss, Chic Stone, Kurt Schaffenberger, Dave Berg, and Marc Swayze to his staff. Otto Binder, an established pulp science-fiction writer, became the chief writer late in 1941.

Fawcett added other comic books to its list—among them *Master Comics*, *Nickel Comics*, and *Wow Comics*—and introduced heroes like Mr. Scarlet, Bulletman, and Radar. But its biggest hit remained Captain Marvel. *Whiz Comics* was selling nearly a half a million copies a month before its first year was out. By 1943, *Captain Marvel Adventures*, containing four Cap yarns per issue, was selling a million copies, and in 1946 the figure approached a million-and-a-half an issue. And that was the year when the magazine was coming out every two weeks.

Master Comics had attempted to succeed where Dell and Major Nicholson failed and make a go of it as a tabloid-size book. They had a superhero, a blonde fellow known as Master Man. Billed as the World's Greatest Hero, he was a dull fellow and didn't even have an alternate identity. Sharing the oversized book with him were Shipwreck Roberts, the White Raja, Frontier Marshall, the Devil's Dagger, and magician El Carim—"whose name printed backwards spells 'miracle.'"

What Fawcett next attempted was a weekly comic book that would sell for a mere five cents. The first issue of *Nickel Comics* appeared with a cover date of May 17, 1940, and the next issue actually appeared two weeks later. The featured hero in the thirty-two-page book was Bulletman. He wore a scarlet tunic, blue sash and boots, and lemon-yellow jodhpurs. His tapered metal helmet made him look something like a bullet. In real life he was a mild-mannered police-lab scientist who had discovered "a germ-destroying serum which transforms him into a hard-muscled, steel-strong giant." Neither *Nickel* nor *Master*, in its original format anyway, clicked. The five-center expired after eight slim issues, and the fifteen-cent *Master* dropped to conventional size and price with its seventh issue. Bulletman whizzed over there and replaced Master Man.

Wow Comics began life late in 1940. Its chief hero was Mr. Scarlet, a satanic-looking crimson avenger drawn originally by Jack Kirby. "Special prosecutor by day, Brian Butler discards his legal robes at midnight to become the mysterious 'Mr. Scarlet,' an underworld legend," explained a caption. "A myth who strikes with merciless reality and brings justice to those who escape the law through its legal loopholes."

➓ ••
MASTER COMICS #25
April 1942
Mac Raboy
Captain Marvel, Jr., soon became the star of *Master*.

➑ •••
CAPTAIN MARVEL, JR. #1
November 1942
Mac Raboy
One of Raboy's many strong covers.

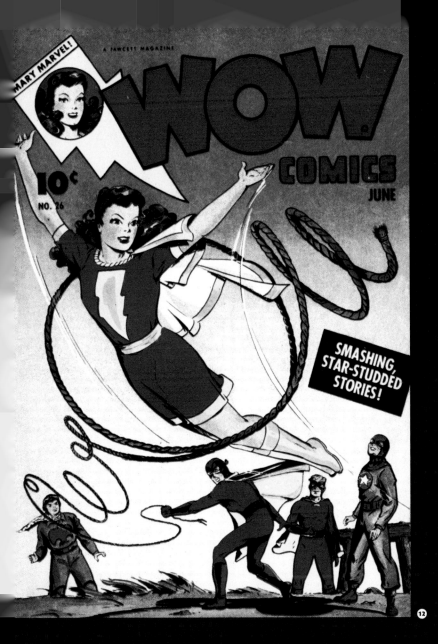

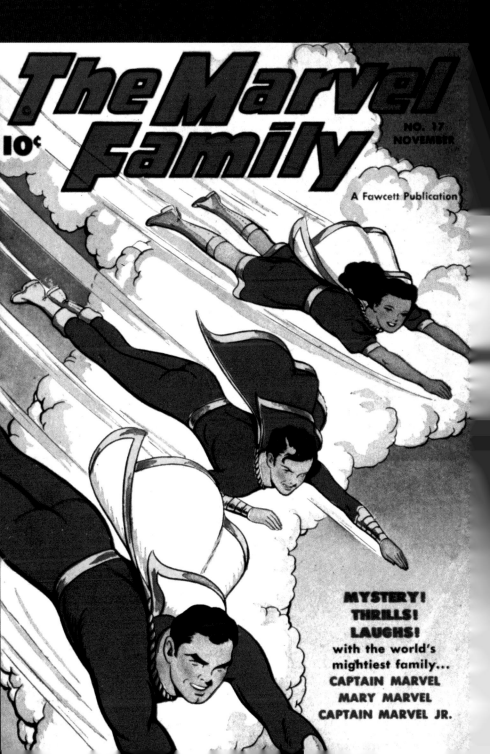

Wow Comics #26
June 1944
Jack Binder
Jack Binder's brother, Otto (formerly pulp writer Eando Binder), was writing most of the Mary Marvel scripts. Her co-stars appear on the cover with Mary Marvel this issue.

The Marvel Family #17
November 1947
C.C. Beck
An additional way to market the Marvels, this title got going in 1945.

Wow Comics #35
April 1945
Jack Binder
Uncle Marvel, a fraud with no super powers whatsoever, was a regular in the Marvel Family saga. He bore some resemblance, in both looks and attitudes, to W.C. Fields.

In *Whiz* #25, a new addition was made to the Marvel family. After an encounter with the odious Captain Nazi, a Germanic superhero created by Hitler, teenage Freddy Freeman was left near death. Billy Batson decided to do something, and he took the dying youth to his old mentor, Shazam. Working a switch on his original trick, Shazam fixed things so that Freddy would become a superhero by shouting, "Captain Marvel!" Since this particular magic phrase wasn't apparently as powerful, Freddy didn't turn into a super adult but rather a super teenager. Decked out in a blue version of the Marvel costume, Captain Marvel, Jr., moved over into *Master Comics* for a long, successful career. Mac Raboy, an impressive artist out of the Chesler shop, drew his first solo adventures. Raboy also drew quite a few effective covers for *Master* and the subsequent *Captain Marvel, Jr.*, comic book.

Lighting struck again a year later. This time it was Mary Marvel, who first flashed into being in *Captain Marvel Adventures* #18. Her real name was Mary Batson and she turned out to be Billy's long-lost sister. By accident, after learning her brother's secret, Mary said, "Shazam!" And—*Whoom!*—she changed, too. "I feel strong—powerful," she exclaimed, not at all disappointed that she'd been transformed into a super teenager and not a full-grown woman. Mary went on to become the star boarder at *Wow Comics* with #9 (January 1943). The chief artist was Jack Binder, Otto's cartoonist brother. Mary Marvel didn't achieve her own magazine until late in 1945. At about

⓱ •••
WOW COMICS #1
Winter 1940
C.C. Beck
Somewhat Satanic in
appearance, Mr. Scarlet was
actually a true-blue do-gooder.

⓲ ••
NATIONAL COMICS #8
February 1941
Lou Fine
National Comics was edited by
Will Eisner, who also created
the updated superhero version
of Uncle Sam.

⓲

that same time, Fawcett also started *The Marvel Family*, a comic book featuring all three of the super Marvels plus Uncle Marvel, a W.C. Fields sort of fraud who'd first surfaced in *Wow*.

The increasing public interest in superheroes meant there was no dearth of entrepreneurs who entered the comic book field. Another of them was Everett M. "Busy" Arnold, a graduate of Brown University who'd worked in the printing business since leaving college. He'd printed the Cook-Mahon Comics Magazine titles and in 1937 he ventured into publishing himself. Probably made cautious by the far from conspicuous success of Cook and Mahon's *Funny Pages* and *Funny Picture Stories*, Arnold made certain he had solvent partners in his own attempt. These included Frank J. Markey, who was an executive with the McNaught Syndicate, and the Cowles family. These latter folks owned the Register & Tribune Syndicate, the Des Moines newspaper of that name, and *Look* magazine. For his editor, Arnold brought in a cartoonist named Ed Cronin. He called his new company the Quality Comics Group, and his first title was *Feature Funnies*, introduced in the autumn of 1937. When it began life, *Feature Funnies* was in the *Famous Funnies* mold and was devoted mainly to reprinting newspaper strips. By early 1940, however, it had changed its name to *Feature Comics* and was showcasing a superhero of its own on its covers. He was the diminutive crimebuster known as the Doll Man, created by Will Eisner and drawn by Lou Fine. By this time, Arnold was using the services of the Eisner-Iger shop.

HIT COMICS #18
December 1941
Reed Crandall
In everyday life, Stormy Foster,
a patriotic superhero also known
as the Great Defender,
worked as a drugstore clerk.
Crandall was noted for his
impressive, illustrative covers
and interior work.

20 ••

CRACK COMICS #5
September 1940
Ed Cronin
The peripatetic Clock was now
hanging out in this magazine.

21 •

CRACK COMICS #32
December 1943
Alex Kotzky
One more captain to add
to the superhero ranks. This
one was Captain Triumph,
created by newspaper cartoonist
Alfred Andriola and associates.

SMASH COMICS #60
August 1945
Jack Cole
After abandoning his creation
for a few years, Jack Cole
returned to him in the
postwar period.

SMASH COMICS #5
December 1939
Paul Gustavson
Bozo was one of the few
robots to star, albeit briefly,
in a comic book.

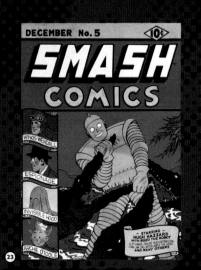

SMASH COMICS #39
January 1943
Reed Crandall
Another impressive Crandall
job, showing the masked
Midnight and his cohorts,
Doc Wacky and Gabby the
talking monkey.

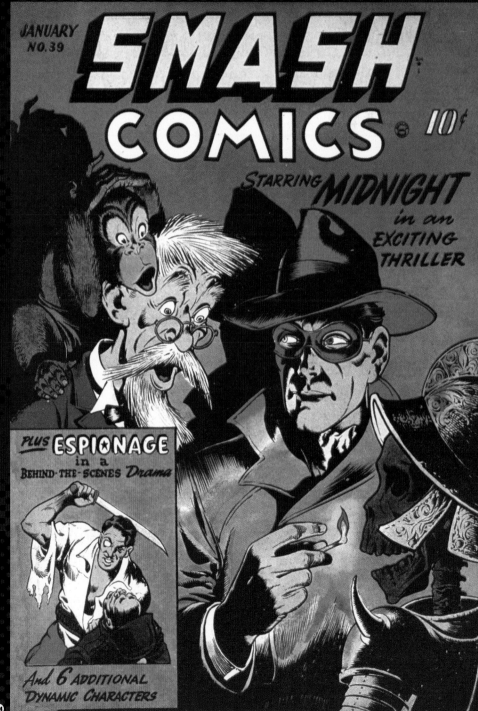

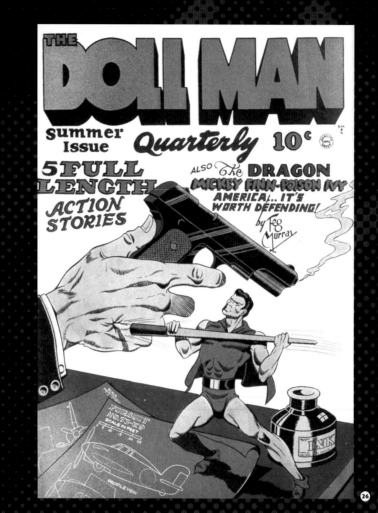

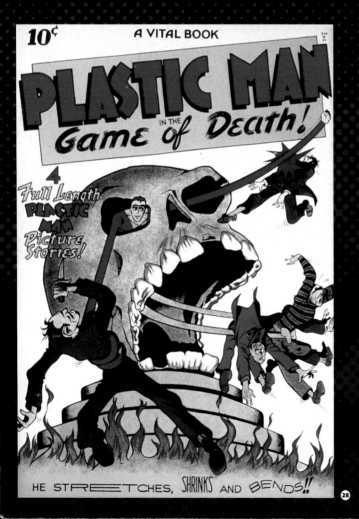

Arnold's next titles were *Smash Comics*, *Crack Comics*, *Hit Comics*, and *National Comics*. These introduced such characters, successful and unsuccessful, as Bozo the Robot, The Ray, Midnight, the Black Condor, The Space Legion, The Red Torpedo, the Clock (the same George E. Brenner masked man who'd been around for several years now), Uncle Sam, Prop Powers, Merlin the Magician, Wonder Boy, Pen Miller, the Red Bee, and Neon the Unknown.

The last two Quality monthlies bowed side by side in the summer of 1941. *Police Comics* featured such as the Firebrand, The Mouthpiece, and the Phantom Lady. The major character, though, was Jack Cole's inventive and irreverent Plastic Man. Later, Will Eisner's Spirit joined the magazine. The character was already two years old by that time, since the weekly *Spirit* Sunday newspaper booklets first appeared in June of 1940. For the comic book reprint of the first story, Eisner added the Spirit's domino mask to the title portrait of his hero. He'd forgotten to do that the first time around. *Military Comics*, also edited by Eisner, offered readers "Stories of the Army and Navy." The undisputed star was Blackhawk, leader of a paramilitary group dedicated to carrying on aerial guerilla warfare against Nazi Germany. It was created by Eisner and drawn by Charles Cuidera. In the second year, the gifted Reed Crandall took over the work art and remained with the feature, off and on, for the next several years.

30 ••
BULLETMAN #6
July 1942
Al Carreno
Though Bulletgirl had become Bulletman's partner some time earlier, she never got her name in the title. Carreno, a caricaturist from Mexico, had drifted into comics in the late 1930s.

Better Publications had begun in 1931, when publisher Ned Pines was asked by a distributor to start a line of ten-cent pulps. With the help of editorial director Leo Margulies, Pines obliged and introduced a multitude of new titles — *Thrilling Detective, Thrilling Love Stories, Thrilling Mystery, Thrilling Wonder Stories, Thrilling Western, The Phantom Detective, G-Men Detective, The Rio Kid, Exciting Detective, Starling Stories, Black Book Detective,* etc. In the late spring of 1939, just as Bat Man was emerging over at *Detective Comics, Black Book* brought forth a similar mystery man named the Black Bat.

Toward the end of the decade, Better ventured into comic books. Their first try, bearing a cover date of November 1939, was *Best Comics.* Next, over the first six months of 1940, came, with titles that might have been expected, *Thrilling Comics, Exciting Comics,* and *Startling Comics.* Actually *Best Comics* was a reprint, though few people had previously seen the recycled ready-print Sunday funny sections that had originally been sold to a few small-town newspapers back in 1936 by an outfit calling itself the Syndicated Features Corp. — no doubt yet another Pines-Margulies business venture. The leading character was the Red Mask, who operated in the jungle and was the closest thing the magazine had to a costumed hero. The rest was intended as humor, stuff such as *Peggy Wow* by newspaper veteran Ray McGill and *Silly Willie* by Loy Byrnes under the anagram byline Roy B. Nyles.

Half of the first issue of *Thrilling* was devoted to the origin of Dr. Strange (not to be confused with the later Marvel mystic). Created by writer Richard Hughes, who was also editing the comic book division products, and drawn initially by Alexander Kostuk, Strange was a gifted scientist who'd invented a compound he called Alosun. This terrific elixir endowed him with a range of powers, including "the ability to soar through the air as if winged." By the fifth issue, no doubt under the influence of pulpwood hero Doc Savage, he changed his name to Doc Strange. Subsequently, he shed his civilian suits for a costume con-

sisting of boots, red T-shirt, and blue riding breeches. Doc Strange was joined in *Thrilling* by the Ghost, the Rio Kid, and the Woman in Red.

Pines' next title, *Exciting Comics*, had an April 1940 cover date and offered a mix of features that included *The Mask*, *Jim Hatfield—Texas Ranger*, and, briefly from the second issue on, *The Space Rovers*. This last was a science-fiction effort drawn by Max Plaisted, who also worked for *Spicy Detective* and illustrated most of the adventures of the hard-boiled Hollywood detective, Dan Turner. In 1936 Plaisted had drawn a black-and-white comic sci-fi filler titled *Zarnak* for

❶ ··
BEST COMICS #4
Howard Sherman
Publisher Ned Pines'
initial try at comic books.

Better's pulpwood *Thrilling Wonder Stories*. The Mask, who wore a hood resembling a sort of horned owl, was actually the Black Bat under a different name and with modified characteristics. Apparently reluctant to annoy DC further, the Pines organization didn't risk calling him anything close to Bat Man when they adapted him to the funny-book medium.

In its ninth issue (May 1941), *Exciting* introduced the Black Terror. A mild-mannered pharmacist, he was yet another superhero who got his powers from a magic potion. In this case, "Bob Benton discovers titanic strength in a solution of formic ethers!" His science might have been a mite shaky, but with his black hair, black domino mask, blue-and-red cape, and black costume adorned with a white skull and crossbones, the Black Terror was certainly one of the more intimidating of all the early superheroes. His sidekick was named simply Tim and wore a junior-size version of the costume. Hughes was again the writer and Elmer Wexler the first artist.

Startling Comics originally starred Captain Future, who bore no resemblance to the Pines pulp hero of the same name created by Edmond Hamilton. The comic book Captain Future was a mild-mannered young research worker who turned himself into a superhero by way of a lab accident. To add to the confusion, the real Captain Future had made one previous comic book appearance, in the first issue of *Exciting*. But, for some reason, he was re-christened Major Mars. His robot associate Grag, however, appeared under his true name. It seems safe to con-

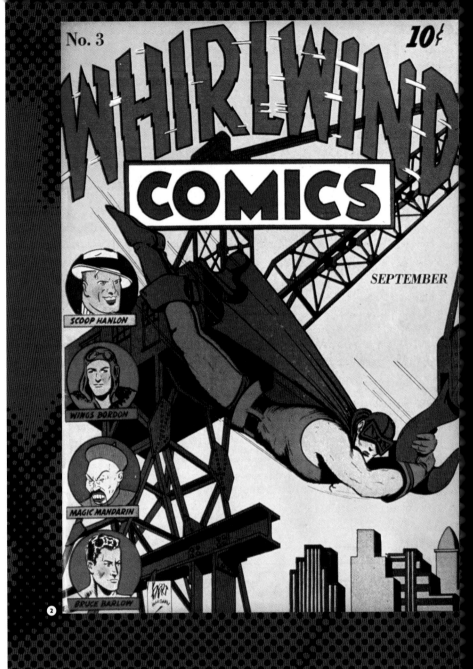

2 ••
WHIRLWIND COMICS #3
September 1940
Bert Whitman
Only artist-packager Whitman knew why a magazine named *Whirlwind* starred a character named The Cyclone.

3 ••
CYCLONE COMICS #1
June 1940
H. L. Parkhurst
The Cyclone would certainly have fit in here, but the leading man was called Tornado Tom.

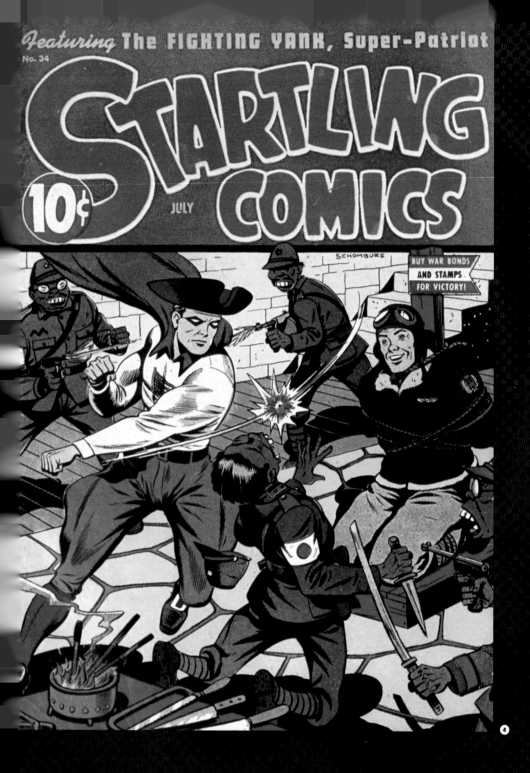

Featuring The FIGHTING YANK, Super-Patriot

No. 34

STARTLING COMICS

10¢ JULY

BUY WAR BONDS AND STAMPS FOR VICTORY!

EXCITING COMICS

10¢ NO.1

EXCITING COMICS #1
April 1940
Max Plaisted
The first and only appearance
of Major Mars and his robot.

EXCITING COMICS #9
May 1941
Elmer Wexler
When the Black Terror wasn't
being a Nemesis of Crime,
he worked in a pharmacy.
But not in that costume.

STARTLING COMICS #34
July 1945
Alex Schomburg
During World War II,
the Fighting Yank, who'd
come to dominate the covers
from #10 on, fought against
both the Japanese and the
German forces.

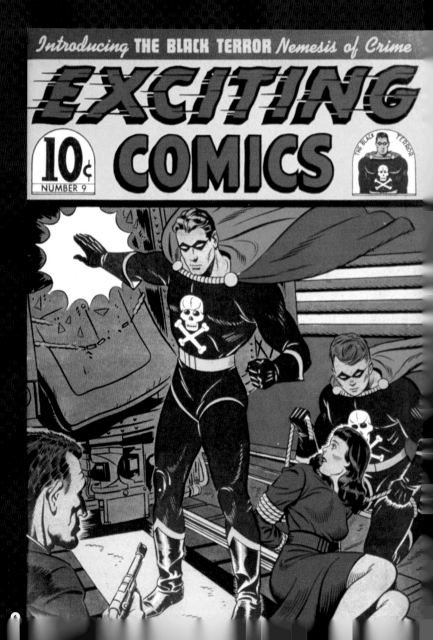

Introducing THE BLACK TERROR *Nemesis of Crime*

EXCITING COMICS

10¢
NUMBER 9

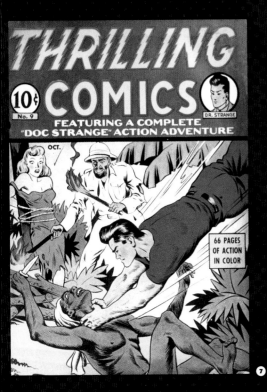

7 ••

THRILLING COMICS #9
October 1940
Alex Schomburg
Doc Strange didn't have much of a costume but very interesting hair.

8 ••

STARTLING COMICS #8
July 1941
Alex Schomburg
The Captain Future seen here stopping a Nazi invasion of America is not to be confused with the pulp-fiction hero of the same name.

clude that Better was having a few problems in trying to convert some of its pulp heroes to the new medium. In *Exciting* #10, Hughes and Wexler again collaborated, this time to create the Fighting Yank. Other characters in the magazine included the Masked Rider, Mystico, and Biff Powers—Big Game Hunter.

Alex Schomburg had worked for Better earlier, but from early 1943 onward, he began producing the majority of their covers. Throughout the 1940s, he drew more than fifty covers for *Thrilling*, nearly as many for *Exciting* and over two dozen for *Startling*. For good measure, he produced another fifty plus covers for their nonfiction book, *Real Life Comics*. For that one, Schomburg depicted such real-life heroes and villains, past and present, as Adolph Hitler, Paul Revere, Sam Houston, Robert Louis Stevenson, General Omar Bradley, and Albert Einstein.

Harry "A" Chesler, now calling himself Dynamic Publications, Inc., had re-entered the publishing field in the autumn of 1941. His new titles included *Yankee Comics*, *Scoop Comics*, and *Punch Comics*. Predominantly serious in tone, they featured heroes such as Yankee Doodle Jones (and his boy partner Dandy), the Enchanted Dagger, Dynamic Man, Major Victory, Mr. "E," the Master Key, Rocketman, Hale the Magician, and the Gay Desperado. Artist Charles Sultan, who was the art director for Chesler during this period, contributed several covers in his best Lou Fine-inspired style. Among the other cover artists were George Tuska, Mac Raboy, and the incomparable Gasparo "Gus" Ricca.

9 ··
HYPER COMICS #1
May 1940
Reg Greenwood
Quite a few ambitious small publishers missed the target entirely. Hyper the Phenomenal was not a hit, and the magazine lasted only two issues—although he, too, wore a fascinating hat.

10 ··
AMERICA'S BEST COMICS #1
February 1942
Alex Schomburg
In this case, the best was none too good.

Yet another pulp publisher who branched out into comics in the early 1940s was Aaron A. Wyn. Under company names such as Magazine Publishers and Periodical House, Wyn had been publishing pulp fiction since 1928. Wyn himself was in charge of titles such as *Ten Detective Ages*, *Flying Aces*, *Ace Sports*, and *Red Seal Western*. His wife, Rose Wyn, supervised *Complete Love*, *Ten Story Love*, and *Secret Agent X*. Their magazines did well, and a 1937 article in *The Literary Digest* mentioned that Wyn was so busy that he had "scant time for supervising the gardening at his estate on Long Island Sound or adding to his collection of antique ivories."

The covers of all the Wyn pulps featured the symbol of a playing card spade with "An ACE Magazine" inscribed across it. The Ace comics, which included *Lightning Comics*, *Super Mystery Comics*, *Banner Comics*, and *Our Flag Comics*, all had the same dingbat on their covers. *Lightning*, originally titled *Sure-Fire Comics*, offered characters such as the speedy "Flash" Lightning, the Raven, Buck Steele, and X—The Phantom Fed, who was a comic book version of the pulp hero Secret Agent X. In *Super Mystery* readers were offered characters such as Vulcan the Volcano Man, "Sky" Smith, Corporal Flint of the RCMP, and Magno the Magnetic Man—"He can draw to himself anything metal and can project himself through space to anything metallic." Among the artists were Harry Lucey and Jim Mooney, who also drew many of the covers. Some of the early back covers carried ads touting the Ace pulps.

11 ••
YANKEE COMICS #2
November 1941
Charles Sultan
Yankee Doodle Jones and Dandy, joined by Major Victory, demonstrate their patriotism.

12 •
BIG SHOT COMICS #17
September 1941
Mart Bailey
The Face was one of the few comic book heroes who did his crime-fighting wearing a tuxedo. His chief weapon was his ugly mask.

13 ••

Dynamic Comics #9
May 1944
Mac Raboy
By the time this cover
appeared, Raboy had long
since ended his association
with Harry "A" Chesler.

14 ••
Sure-Fire Comics #3
September 1940
Harry Lucey
"Flash" Lightning, who later
changed his name to Lash
Lightning, was one of several
Golden Age heroes who looked
a good deal like Alex Raymond's
Flash Gordon.

MLJ Magazines, Inc. also got going during this period. Less formal that the movie studio MGM, the MLJ company took its name from the initials of the first names of its proprietors, men who had experience in pulp publishing and magazine distribution. They were Morris Coyne, Louis Silberkleit, and John Goldwater, who entered the burgeoning funny-book field together at the end of 1939. The artwork and scripts for their earliest issues were provided by the Chesler shop.

While talented people did work for Chesler, it's evident he didn't send in his first team to turn out MLJ's new line. It got off to a somewhat shaky start with *Blue Ribbon Comics* (November 1939), whose star was not a costumed superhero but a dog. Billed as the Wonder Dog, Rang-A-Tang gnawed on a villain's wrist on the cover and led off the issue with a six-page adventure.

By the fourth issue, MLJ had quit Chesler and hired some of his better staffers, including Charles Biro, Bob Wood, and Mort Meskin, away from him. New characters such as Hercules, the Fox, the Green Falcon, and Ty-Gor were added. The ninth issue added Mr. Justice, created by writer Joe Blair and artist Sam Cooper as a rival to DC's ghostly Spectre.

❷⓿ ••
**SUPER-MYSTERY COMICS
#14 (V3 #2)**
July 1942
Frank Harry
Three heroes battle a consortium of green ne'er-do-wells.

❷❶ ••
**SUPER-MYSTERY COMICS #13
(V3 #1)**
April 1942
Joe Gallagher
Magno and Davey rush to save a young woman from the poisoned claws of the Cobra.

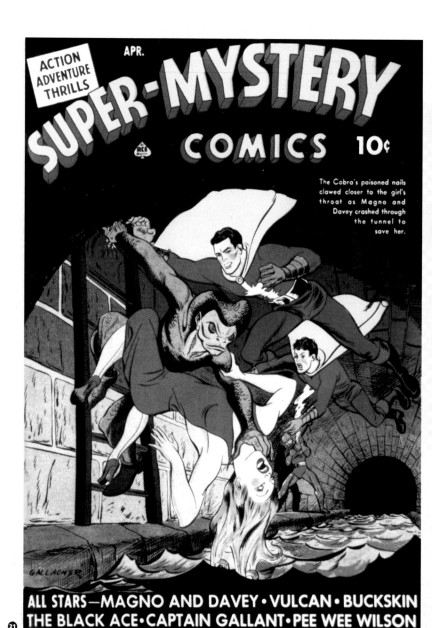

100

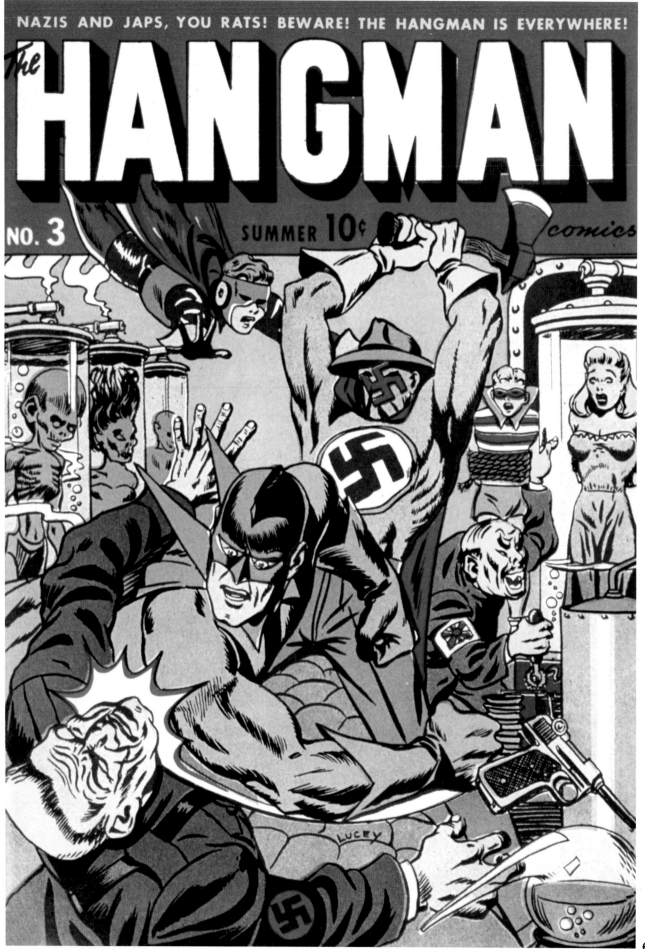

27 ••
HANGMAN #3
Summer 1942
Harry Lucey
Roy and Dusty help the
Hangman thwart a rather
puzzling Nazi plot.

28 ••
PEP COMICS #16
June 1941
Irv Novick
A favorite opponent of the
Shield and Dusty was the Vulture.

The second MLJ title was *Top-Notch Comics*, the eventual home of characters such as the Wizard, The Firefly, and the Black Hood. *Pep Comics* came next, with the Shield, also known as "the G-Man Extraordinary," Jack Cole's vindictive The Comet, Kayo Ward, and Inspector Bentley of Scotland Yard. When the Comet was killed by gangsters' bullets, the even more ruthless Hangman replaced him in #17.

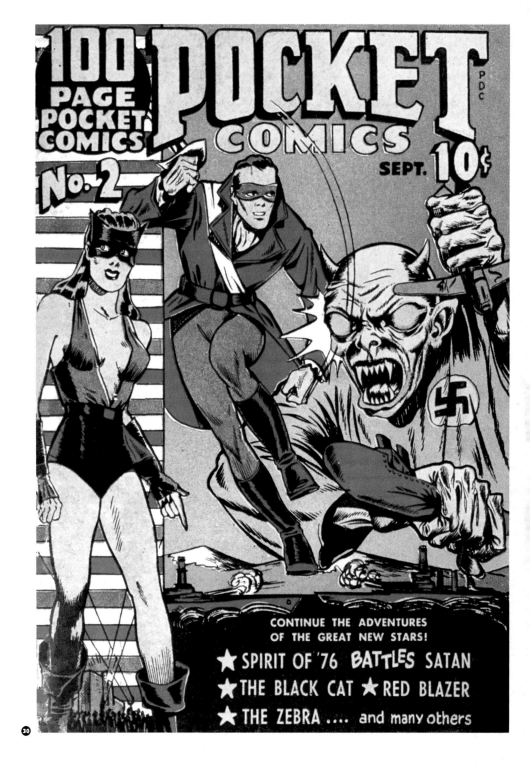

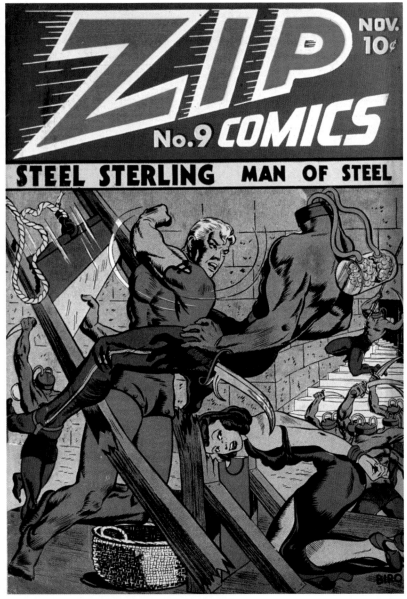

29 ••
Zip Comics #9
November 1940
Charles Biro
Decapitation of pretty women
was a frequent motif with Biro.

30 ••
Pocket Comics #2
September 1941
Al Gabrielle
This unsuccessful digest
introduced the successful lady
crimefighter, the Black Cat.
In everyday life, she was
Linda Turner, redheaded
Hollywood movie star.

The fourth monthly from MLJ was *Zip Comics*. The leading superhero there was Steel Sterling, a joint effort by artist Charles Biro and writer Abner Sundell, who was also the magazine's editor. Since Biro had been doing cute comedy fillers for the Chesler shop until a few months earlier, he was not completely at home with straight adventure. But he had a strong sense of action and his early pages, though often crudely drawn, had movement and life. Biro's effective techniques for grabbing and holding the readers' attention would always remain several paces ahead of his actual drawing ability. Besides Steel Sterling, *Zip* offered other costumed heroes—the Scarlet Avenger, Mr. Satan, Black Jack, and the Web.

The deluge of new companies and titles continued through the early 1940s. Crestwood offered *Prize Comics*, with the Black Owl, Dick Briefer's Frankenstein, and the Green Lama—another pulp character adapted to comic books. Vincent Sullivan left DC to edit Columbia Comics' *Big Shot Comics*, the home of Skyman, the Face, Captain Devildog, Marvelo, and Sparky Watts. He brought with him artists and writers such as Fred Guardineer, Creig Flessel, Ken Ernst, and Gardner Fox.

The Hillman Company, a pioneer in paperback books, introduced *Air Fighters*, which later changed its name to that of its youthful leading hero, *Airboy*. Alfred Harvey, who'd worked for Victor Fox, joined with some of his relatives to produce *Speed Comics*, *Green*

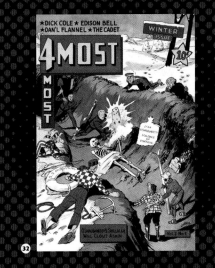

32 •

4 MOST #5 (V2 #1)
Winter 1942
John Jordan
An old-fashioned boys'
book sort of cover.
Except for that skeleton.

33 ••

4-FAVORITES #8
December 1942
Louis Ferstadt
Ace's answer to DC's
All Star Comics, with a cover by
the incomparable Ferstadt.

Hornet, and *Champ Comics* with characters such as Captain Freedom, Shock Gibson, and the Black Cat, who became one of the most popular of female crimefighters. Joe Simon and Jack Kirby, usually under the penname of Jon Henri, provided many covers, as did Alex Schomburg.

The Curtis Publishing Company of Philadelphia, publisher of both *The Saturday Evening Post* and *Ladies' Home Journal*, also went unobtrusively into the comics business in 1940. Calling itself Novelty Press, Inc., and operating out of editorial offices on West 52nd Street in Manhattan, Curtis issued *Target Comics* and *Blue Bolt*. The former featured Carl Burgos' White Streak, Basil Wolverton's eccentric Spacehawk, and Bob Woods' the Target and the Targeteers. The hero of the second title was Blue Bolt, a superhero who represented the first collaboration of the formidable team of Joe Simon and Jack Kirby. Bob Davis' Dick Cole was also aboard and was one of the few schoolboy heroes to be found in American comic books. Both a writer and an artist, Bob Davis had sold stories to the detective pulps and in the early 1930s drawn a short-lived newspaper strip about suave detective Philo Vance.

Also available on the newsstands of the early 1940s were Nita Publications' *Whirlwind Comics*, which starred the Cyclone, Bilbara Publishing's *Cyclone Comics*, which starred Tornado Tom, Hyper's *Hyper Mystery*, which starred Hyper the Phenomenal and dozens more.

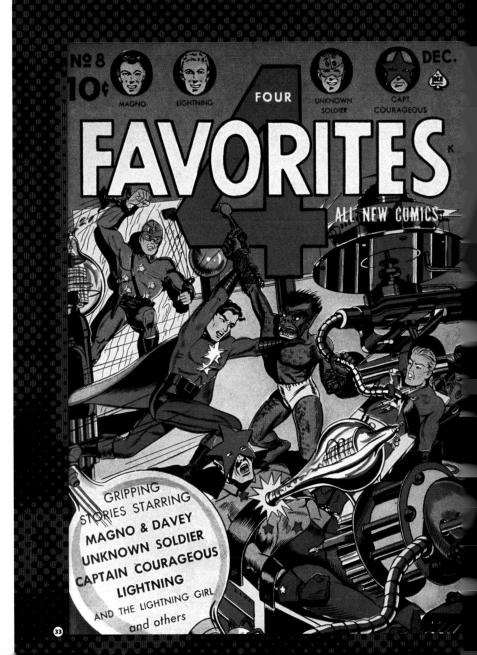

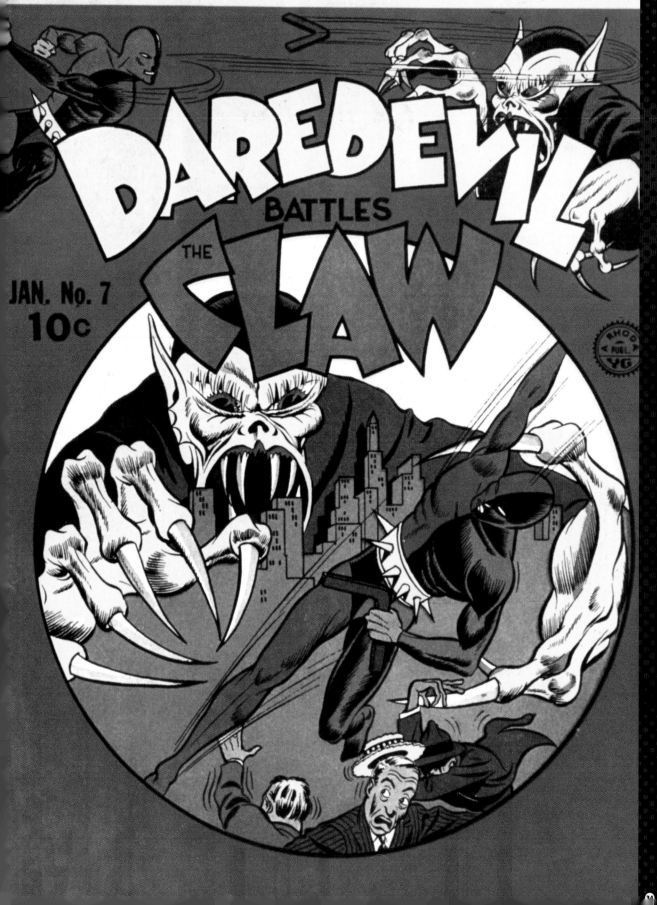

SILVER STREAK COMICS

DAREDEVIL BATTLES THE CLAW

JAN. No. 7
10c

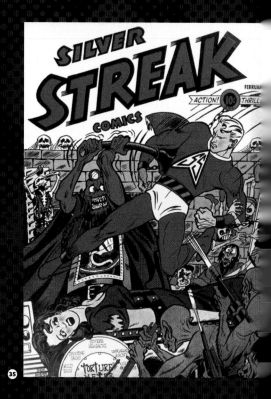

35

· ·
[D]AREDEVIL #6
[D]ecember 1941
[Ch]arles Biro

· ·
[SI]LVER STREAK COMICS #10
[M]ay 1941
[B]ob Wood
[W]ood was a graduate of the
[C]hesler shop, as was Charles
[B]iro with whom he'd soon
[b]e teaming up to edit several
[n]ew comic books.

· · ·
[D]AREDEVIL BATTLES HITLER #1
[Ju]ly 1941
[W]oodro (Wood and Biro)
[A]s America got closer to
[e]ntering World War II, comic
[b]ooks paid increasing attention
[to] Hitler and the Axis powers.
[T]he first issue of Daredevil's
[o]wn magazine was packaged
[by] Funnies, Inc., and pitted the
[c]haracters from *Silver Streak Comics*
[a]gainst assorted Axis enemies.

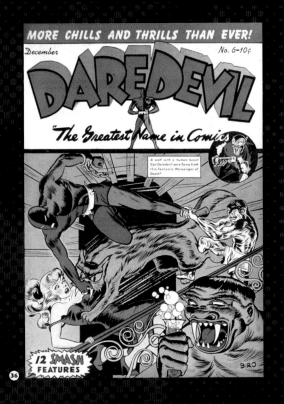

36

37

38

39

· · ·
SILVER STREAK COMICS #8
March 1941
Jack Cole
"Wow! What An Exciting Number
This Is!" Another exuberant
and eye-catching effort by Cole.

· ·
DAREDEVIL COMICS #11
June 1942
Charles Biro
One of Biro's most memorable
covers. Readers felt compelled
to read the story inside in
hopes of finding out how the
young woman got into this
unusual predicament.

40

By 1944, the comic book industry was thriving, and almost any publisher who could get paper—rationed at the time—was making money. In that year, DC was publishing nineteen different titles and running up combined monthly sales of over 8,500,000 copies. In 1945, Fawcett, with eight titles, reported sales of 4,500,000 each month. That same year MLJ's five titles had combined sales of nearly 2,000,000 monthly, and Quality's nine titles sold over 1,500,000.

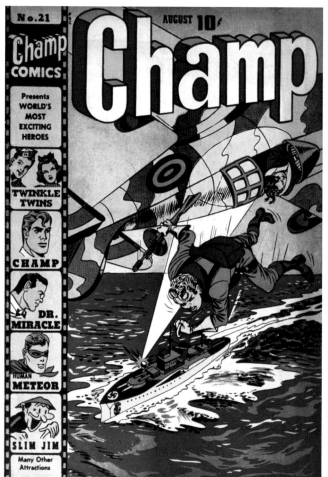

41 ··
SPEED COMICS #19
June 1942
Joe Simon & Jack Kirby
The magazine returned to the
regular format fairly soon.

42 ··
CHAMP COMICS #21
August 1941
Joe Simon & Jack Kirby

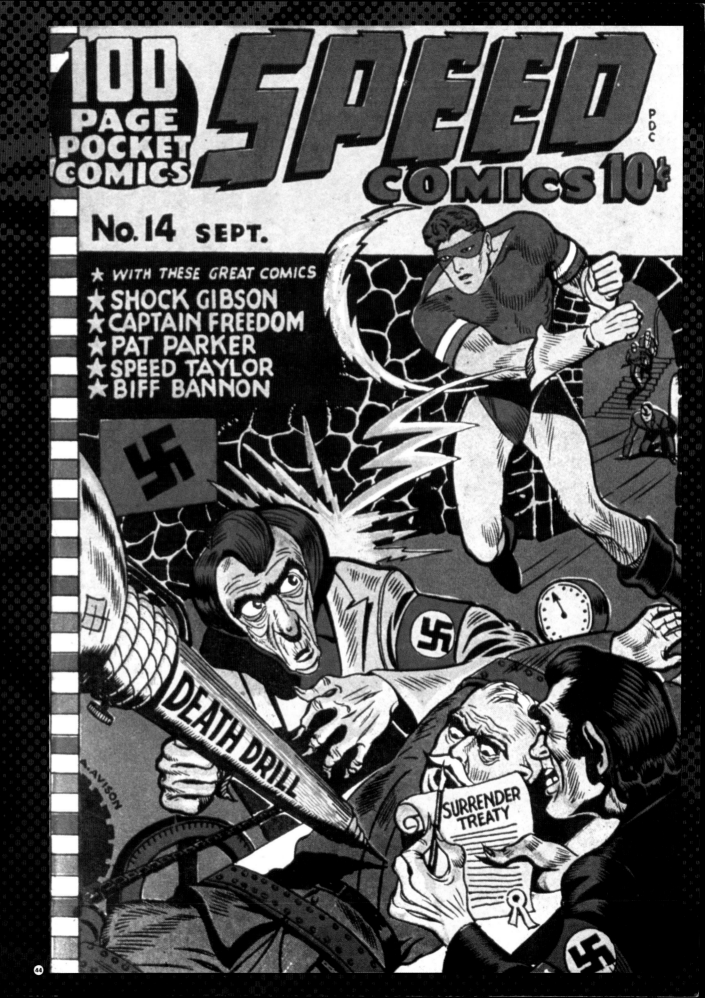

45 ··
TARGET COMICS #6
July 1940
Unknown
The White Streak doing
some impressive leaping.

46 ···
TARGET COMICS #7
August 1940
Basil Wolverton
Wolverton's only serious
Golden Age cover.

47 ··
TARGET COMICS #18 (V2 #6)
August 1941
Bob Wood
Bob Wood and Bob Kane
were both assisted by George
Roussos at this time. Hence,
the similarity in their work.

48 ··
TARGET COMICS #34 (V3 #10)
December 1942
Harold DeLay
Toning down its image and
becoming more sedate inside,
Target added adaptations of
the classics to the lineup.
They also dropped Wolverton's
flamboyant *Spacehawk*.

49 ··
TARGET COMICS #23 (V2 #11)
January 1942
John Jordan
Apparently the villain that
Kit Carter the Cadet is facing
hadn't seen this trick pulled
dozens of times in the movies.

A publisher usually made six cents on every ten-cent comic book sold. On a title like *Captain Marvel Adventures*, Fawcett would take in about $78,000 per issue for a total of around $936,000 a year. DC's gross for 1945, when they'd increased their roster to over twenty-one titles, was in the neighborhood of $6,500,000 and that doesn't include profits from toys, radio shows, movies, and other forms of licensing and merchandising. Sales figures like these are what inspired the continuing expansion of the comic book industry during World War II and after.

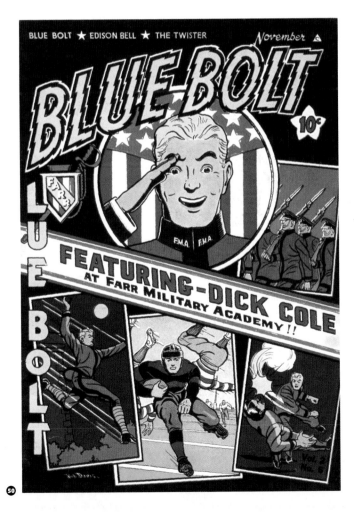

50 ••
Blue Bolt #18 (V2 #6)
November 1941
Bob Davis
The school song at Farr Military Academy was "We'll Always be Near to Farr."

51 ••
Blue Bolt #16 (V2 #4)
September 1941
Bob Davis
A simple and effective poster-style cover.

Throughout the early and middle 1940s, the number of new comic books to be found on the newsstands continued to grow. Some publishers became millionaires, others failed completely. Entrepreneurs and packagers came and went, all dreaming of success.

Cartoonist Bert Whitman, for example, had done some work for Major Nicholson on *New Fun*. In 1940, with the comic book business flourishing, he set up a shop to produce stories and art for publishers such as Frank Temerson. Among his employees were Jack Kirby, Irwin Hasen, George Storm, and Frank Robbins. Whitman put together titles such as *Whirlwind Comics*, *Crash Comics*, and *Green Hornet Comics*. None and Whitman's titles did well, and he quit packaging to concentrate on just drawing and writing for comic books. But he'd licensed the radio hero, Green Hornet and when he quit running his shop, he sold the license to the Harvey comics outfit. He later maintained that he made more money by selling the rights to the Green Hornet than anybody ever made publishing comic books about him.

Cat-Man, who'd first appeared in *Crash*, fared somewhat better in his own title from a new publisher and managed to survive for six years. But many titles turned out to be ephemeral. *Captain Fearless* lasted two issues, *Superworld Comics* made it through three, and *Bang-Up Comics* also never got beyond its third issue. *Choice Comics*, put together by Jerry Iger, only reached #3, as did its companion *Great Comics*. *Blazing Comics*, starring the mysterious Green Turtle, published five issues, *Captain Flight Comics* made it through eleven.

As the 1940s progressed, some old standby reprint magazines tossed out most if not all of their comic-strip features in hopes of competing with the waves of superhero and costumed crimefighter comics. *Popular* added characters such as The Voice—an invisible detective, the Masked Pilot, Dr. Hormone—don't ask, Professor Supermind and Son. *Super* made room for Magic Morro, foreign correspondent Jack Wander, and South Sea adventurer Jim Ellis. Over at *Crackajack*, they added Ellery Queen, Stratosphere Jim, and The Owl. And the venerable *The Funnies* tried everything from a very odd superhero named Phantasmo to an adaptation of radio-hero Captain Midnight's adventures. Both *Popular* and *Super* eventually returned to a reprint format. *The Funnies* turned into *New Funnies*, with animated cartoon characters like Andy Panda and kids' book characters like Raggedy Ann. *Crackajack* folded after its forty-third issue early in 1942.

Street & Smith did fairly well with their *Shadow* comic book and with *Super Magician*, both scripted by Walter Gibson. But titles like *Red Dragon* and *Ghost Busters*, even with contributions from artists such as Bob Powell, Joe Maneely, and Edd Cartier, failed. At the end of the 1940s, S&S quit printing comic books and pulp magazines.

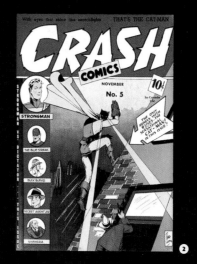

❶ ··
CRASH COMICS #1
May 1940
Bert Whitman
Strongman was yet another of the optimistic heroes who emerged in the early 1940s only to fail.

❷ ··
CRASH COMICS #5
November 1940
Bert Whitman
Unlike Cat-Man (seen here), *Crash* didn't have nine lives. It succumbed for good with this issue.

CAT-MAN COMICS #1
May 1941
Charles M. Quinlan
The unkillable Cat-Man
returned with a new publisher
and a title of his own.

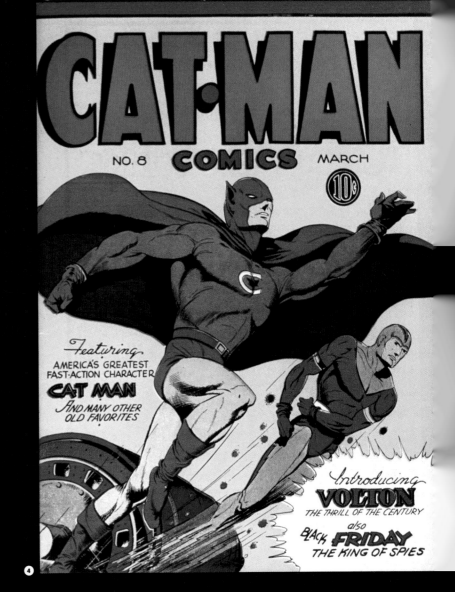

"America's Most Thrilling, Fast-Action Adventure Stories!"

4

CAT-MAN COMICS #8
March 1942
Ray Willner

5

CAT-MAN COMICS #3
July 1941
Charles M. Quinlan

IRON VIC
One-shot 1940
Bernard Dibble

Vic began life as a Superman imitator but soon forgot all about that and became a professional baseball player and then a U.S. Marine. He ended up as a backup character in *Tip Top Comics*.

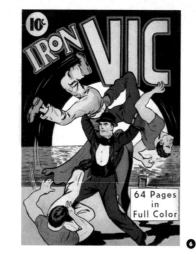

CRACKAJACK FUNNIES #36
June 1941
Frank Thomas

The Owl acquired a female partner called Owl Girl, but she never shared a cover with him.

CRACKAJACK FUNNIES #34
April 1941
Frank Thomas

Crackajack added the Batman-like Owl in hopes of boosting circulation.

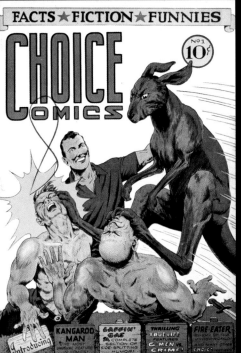

9

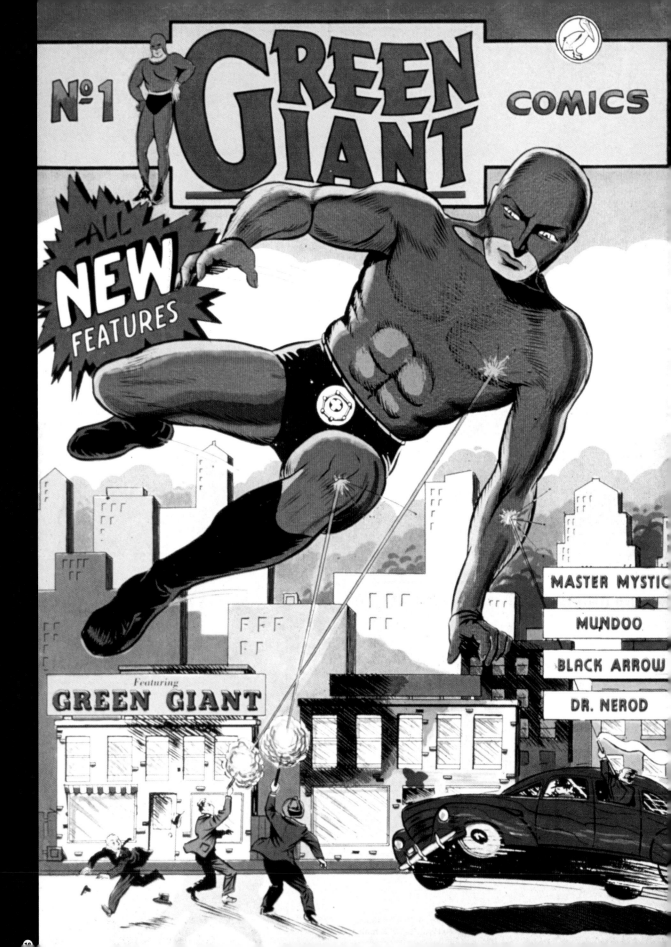

Featuring SKY WIZARD MASTER of SPACE

MIRACLE Comics
APRIL NO. 3
10 CENTS

ALSO: DASH DIXON • BLANDA—JUNGLE QUEEN • DUSTY DOYLE
THE SCORPION • PINKIE PARKER • GHOST RIDER • K-7

11 ••
MIRACLE COMICS #3
April 1940
Unknown

ACTION! THRILLS! ADVENTURE!
ROCKET Comics
HURRICANE HART High Seas Hellion
RED ROBERTS The Electro Man
THE STEEL SHARK Deep Sea Raider
BUZZARD BARNES and His Sky Devils
MARCH 10¢
SMASH FEATURE: ROCKET RILEY PRINCE OF THE PLANETS

13 ••
ROCKET COMICS #1
March 1940
John. R. Flanagan

14 ••
BANG-UP COMICS #2
March 1942
Rick Yager
The result of a Chicago-based
publisher approaching some
Chicago-based cartoonists and
asking them if they'd like to help
create a new magazine. When the
publisher asked what the going
rate per page was, they told him
one several times higher. He
paid it, but, unfortunately, the
magazine only lasted three issues.

12 ••
AIR FIGHTERS #14 (V2 #2)
November 1943
Fred Kida
Hillman did much better with
this one, especially after they'd
asked Charles Biro to invent
some new characters. That's one
of them, Airboy, sprawled on
the floor and temporarily bested
by the feisty Valkyrie.

AIR FIGHTERS COMICS
NOVEMBER Latest War Thrills! 10¢
IT'S VALKYRIE, AIRBOY-- AND THE AIRMAIDENS ARE WITH ME!! NOT EVEN SKYWOLF, THE IRON ACE, BLACK ANGEL OR FLYING DUTCHMAN CAN SAVE YOU NOW!

SUPER ACTION WONDERS — ADVENTURES!

16 • • •

SUPERWORLD COMICS #1

April 1940

Frank R. Paul

Publisher Hugo Gernsback had invented the science-fiction pulp with *Amazing Stories* back in the 1920s. He apparently had no idea as to what a successful comic book should be. Young readers didn't take to characters such as Mitey Powers, the Invisible Avenger, and Hip Knox the Super Hypnotist.

17 • •

THE FUNNIES #57

July 1941

E.C. Stoner

As sales on reprint magazines waned, they made efforts to compete with their flashier competitors. But not even Captain Midnight could save *The Funnies*.

18 • •

CLUE #2

February 1943

Charles Biro

The Boy King never fared as well as Airboy. But Biro certainly provided a nice hard-sell cover for Hillman.

15 • •

CAPTAIN FEARLESS COMICS #2

September 1941

Charles M. Quinlan

A few years later, Davy Crockett enjoyed a much more impressive career wearing a similar hat.

Captain Flight Comics #6
January 1946

Iger Studio

Much more interesting than anything to be found inside, this cover can provide hours of entertainment. You might try to speculate as to exactly what events led up to the situation pictured here. Why, for instance, are those fellows in the hoods getting ready to burn the blonde at the stake? Did she set fire to that house in the background? Is that her plane that's burning? If so, why was she piloting it dressed like she is? Who's in the airplane that's strafing the fellows in the hoods? Is that Captain Flight himself? If so, why does he have hearts emblazoned on his ship? Is this some sort of Valentine's Day activity that got out of hand? Well, you get the idea.

Captain Flight Comics #2
May 1944

Charles M. Quinlan

The Jerry Iger shop recycled some old stuff from *Wings Comics* and *Flight Comics* to come up with the contents for this magazine.

21 ••

MAD HATTER #2

September-October 1946

Mort Leav

Even borrowing a name from Lewis Carroll didn't help.

22 •

GHOST BREAKERS #2

December 1948

Bob Powell

Dr. Neff's own magazine survived for only two issues.

23 •

BLAZING COMICS #3

September 1944

Chu Hing

Did anyone actually expect a magazine staring a hero called the Green Turtle to succeed?

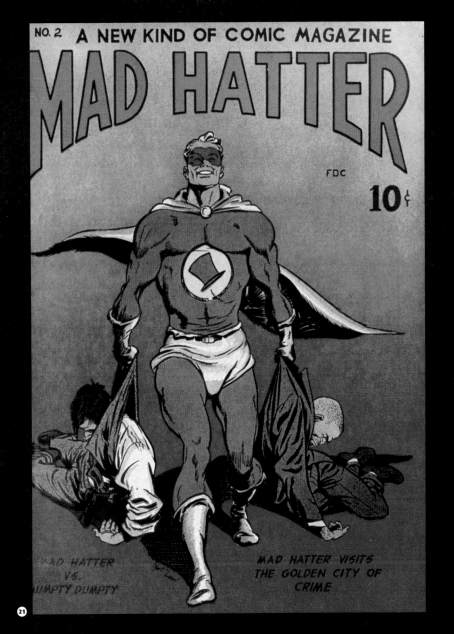

24 •

CAPTAIN WIZARD #1

1946

John Giunta

A talented but ill-fated artists Giunta drew quite a few interesting covers for uninteresting magazines.

25 •

SPOOK COMICS #1

1946

John Giunta

Another title packaged by Bernard Baily, who employed some excellent artists—such as John Giunta and his assistant, the young Frank Frazetta.

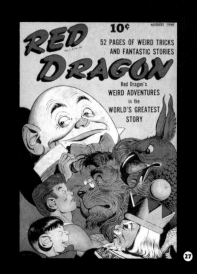

The postwar years saw hopeful shoestring publishers still trying to make a go of it with costumed
heroes, but magazines like *Mad Hatter*, *Captain Wizard*,
Golden Lad, and *Atoman* didn't find success. It would be
new genres—especially crime, horror and romance-
that would keep the business going into the 1950s.

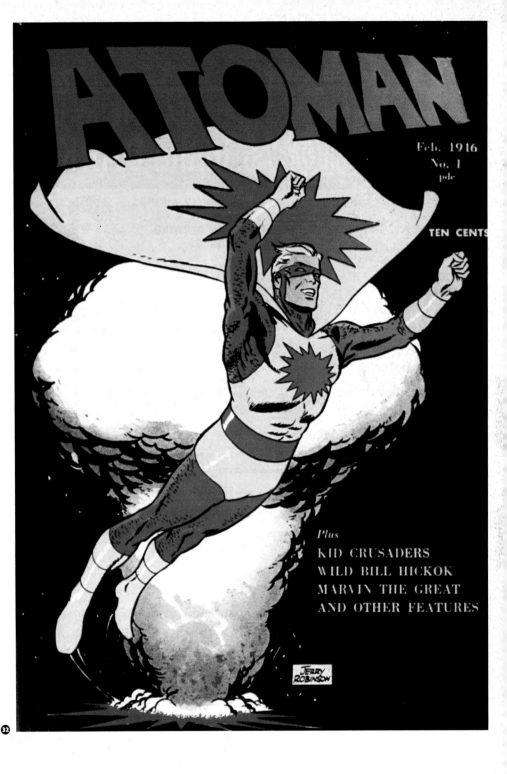

31 •
TREASURE #4
December 1945
Bernard Baily
Co-creator of DC's *Spectre*,
Baily had his own shop by this
time and was packaging this
title. On the cover he drew his
own character, Dr. Styx.

32 ••
ATOMAN #1
February 1946
Jerry Robinson
One more superhero
inspired by the atomic bomb.

Jack Kirby, Alex Schomburg, Gus Ricca, L.B. Cole

Jack Kirby. Kirby (1917-1994) was called the "King of Comics." And certainly he was one of the most prolific, successful, and influential of comic book artists. Over the years, alone or in partnership with others, he created Captain America, The Boy Commandos, The Fantastic Four, Manhunter, Thor, The Hulk, Fighting American, etc.

His real name was Jacob Kurtzberg and he was born on New York's Lower East Side. After a spell in animation and low-level newspaper syndicate work, he moved into comic books in the late 1930s. There was a freshness and energy to his early work. He had a brash, noisy style, that of a tough street kid trying to mask his grace. Kirby was especially good at the figure in action. His characters moved—sometimes the panels couldn't contain them—and when they slugged each other, you felt it. His heroes were brawlers, more stuntmen than matinée idols. His fight scenes blended the violent with the lyrical, a mixture of wrestling and ballet that worked. Sort of like choreographed saloon brawls.

Although his earliest work was done solo, with Kirby pencilling, inking, and, sometimes, scripting, his most memorable work during the Golden Age was done in collaboration with Joe Simon. They usually worked with Kirby pencilling and Simon inking, or at least supervising the inking when the workload got too heavy.

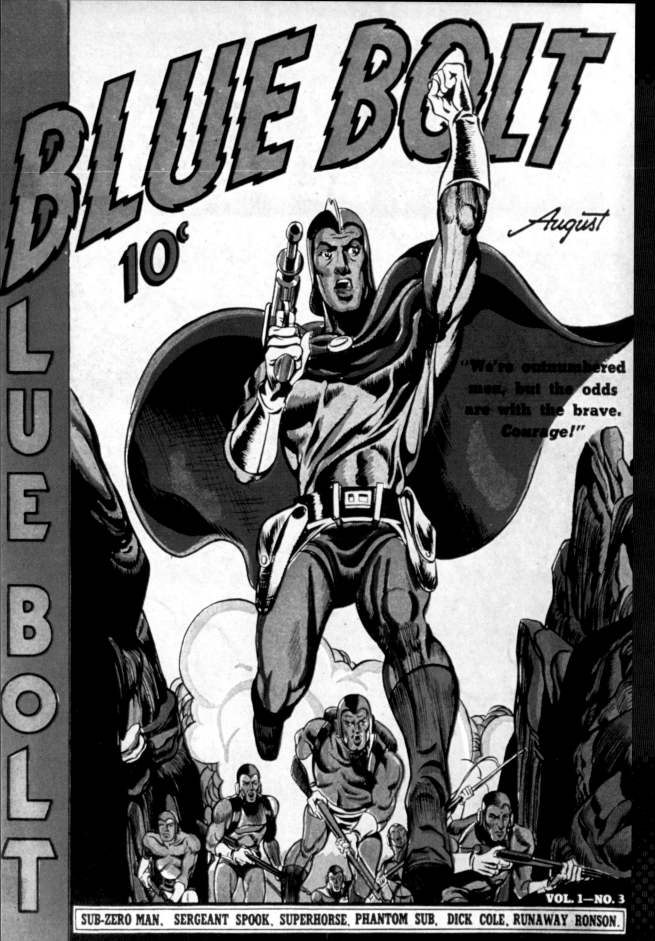

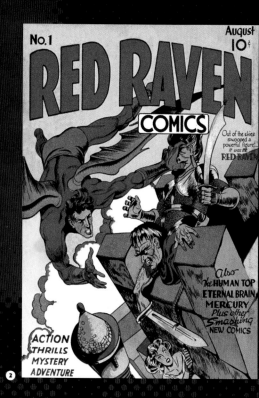

1 ··
BLUE BOLT #3
August 1940
Joe Simon and Jack Kirby
The first collaboration
between Kirby and Joe Simon.

2 ···
RED RAVEN #1
August 1940
Jack Kirby
The only issue.

❸ ··
CAPTAIN AMERICA #7
October 1941
Joe Simon and Jack Kirby
The team's first big hit.

❹ ··
CHAMP #20
July 1941
Joe Simon and Jack Kirby

❺ ··
CHAMPION #8
June 1940
Jack Kirby
The Human Meteor looked
better on Kirby's covers than
he ever did inside the book.

❻ ··
CHAMPION #10
August 1940
Jack Kirby

❼ ··
CLUE COMICS #15
May 1947
Joe Simon and Jack Kirby
The Gunmaster to the rescue.

127

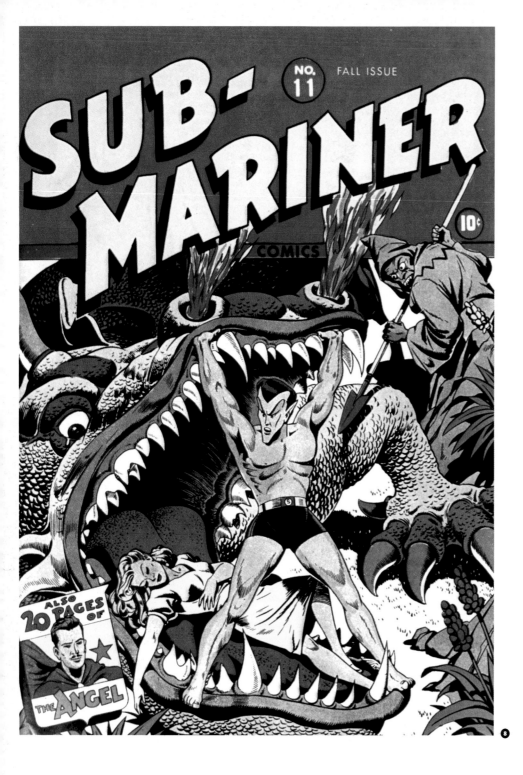

Alex Schomburg. Comic books only occupied him for a decade or so, from the late 1930s to the late 1940s. But in that decade or so Schomburg drew well over five hundred covers, an average of one a week. The usual pay rate was about sixty-five dollars per cover.

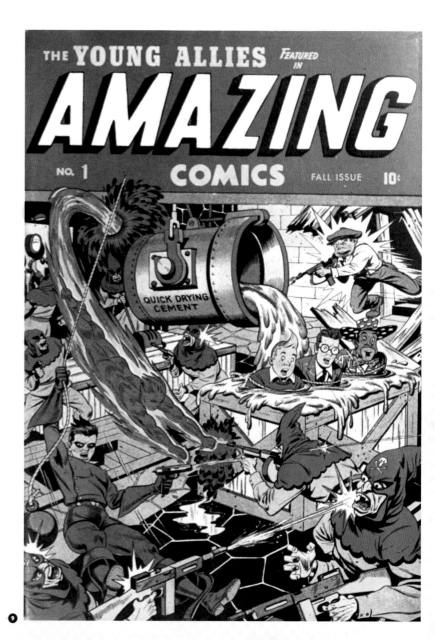

8 ··
SUB-MARINER #11
Fall 1943
Alex Schomburg

9 ··
AMAZING COMICS #1
Fall 1944
Alex Schomburg

Born in Puerto Rico in 1905, he had resettled in Manhattan by the early 1920s. He and three of his brothers were soon operating a successful commercial-art studio. By the next decade, he'd moved from advertising to illustrating for pulps. He did quite a bit of work for the Pines-Margulies titles—*Thrilling Adventure*, *Thrilling Detective*, *Thrilling Wonder Stories*. As the 1930s ended, he discovered comic books.

His most memorable efforts were for Marvel (then known as Timely) in the years just before and during World War II. Schomburg became an expert at depicting Captain America, the Human Torch, and Sub-Mariner, singly or as a team, in the most complex and improbable situations. His spectacular and intricate covers appeared on *Marvel Mystery Comics*, *Human Torch*, *Sub-Mariner*, *All Winners*, *The Young Allies*, and just about every other Timely title.

He also turned out covers for *Thrilling Comics*, *Exciting Comics*, and *Black Terror* and Harvey titles such as *Speed Comics*, *All-New*, and *The Green Hornet*. The Harvey covers usually came with a two-page printed explanation inside, called *The Story Behind the Cover*—and the writer who could fit the whole story of a typical Schomburg cover into that limited space was indeed a master of compression.

After leaving comics in the 1950s, he devoted his time to illustrating books and science-fiction magazines such as *Isaac Asimov's* and *Amazing Stories*. He died in 1998.

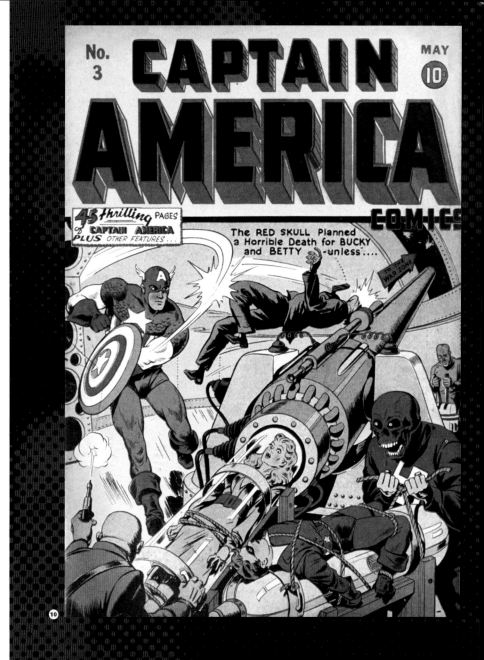

10 •••
CAPTAIN AMERICA #3
May 1941
Alex Schomburg
The Schomburg variations on Captain America, Bucky, and the villainous Red Skull.

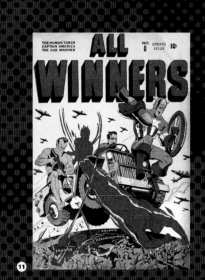

11 ••
ALL WINNERS #8
Spring 1943
Alex Schomburg
Yet another use for a Jeep.

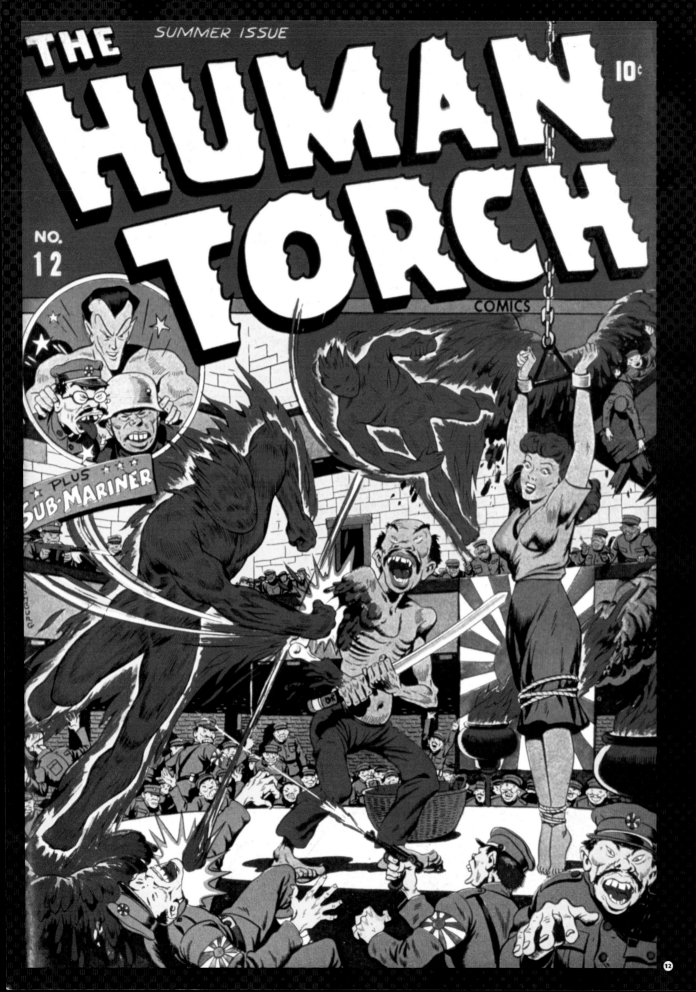

12 ••
HUMAN TORCH #12
Summer 1943
Alex Schomburg

13 ••
DARING #10
Winter 1944
Alex Schomburg
Schomburg became the
Hieronymus Bosch of comic
book covers during World
War II. He was turning out
one or two of these intricate
battle scenes each week.

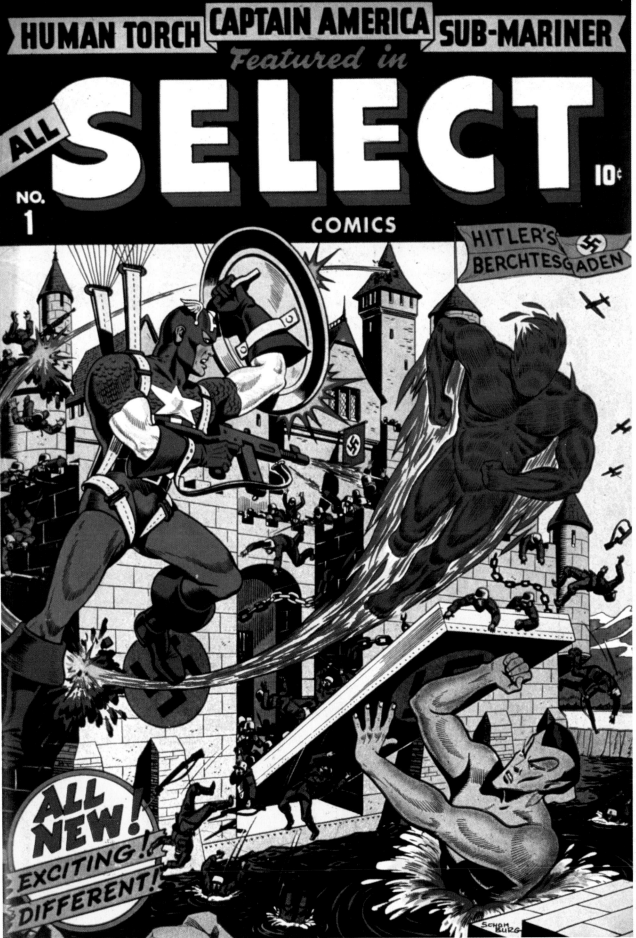

14 ••
Marvel Mystery Comics #52
February 1944
Alex Schomburg

15 ••
All Select Comics #1
Fall 1943
Alex Schomburg

16 ••
EXCITING COMICS #28
August 1943
Alex Schomburg
Schomburg's covers for
the Pines' magazines were
usually simpler.

17 ••
AMERICA'S BEST COMICS #9
April 1944
Alex Schomburg

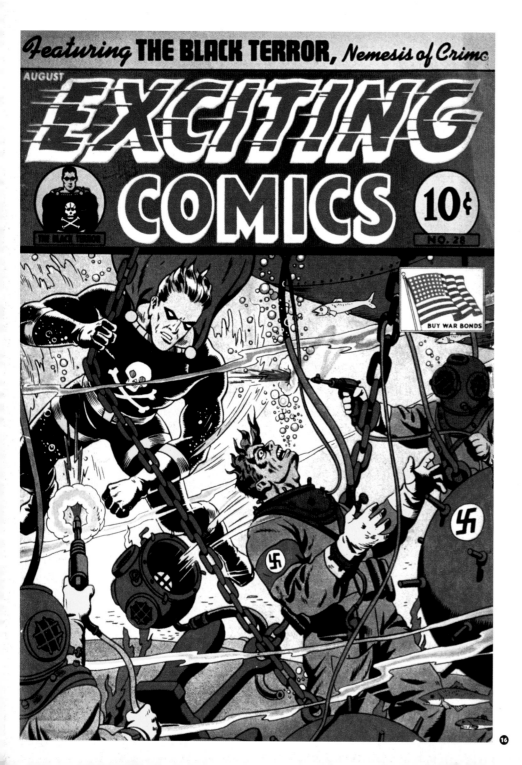

18 ••
FIGHTING YANK #23
February 1948
Alex Schomburg
Different villains for the
postwar covers.

Wonder Comics #6
August 1945
Alex Schomburg
This character was called
the Grim Reaper. Instead of a
scythe, he used a machine gun.

Wonder Comics #20
October 1948
Alex Schomburg
Schomburg used the penname
Xela on most of his airbrushed
postwar covers.

Cat-Man Comics #24
May 1944
Alex Schomburg
Schomburg's lone cover for
this magazine.

Mystery Comics #1
1944
Alex Schomburg

All-New Comics #8
May 1944
Alex Schomburg
Originally called Red Rover,
this hero became Captain
Red Rover. He appeared only
on All-New covers and in
the short text stories inside.

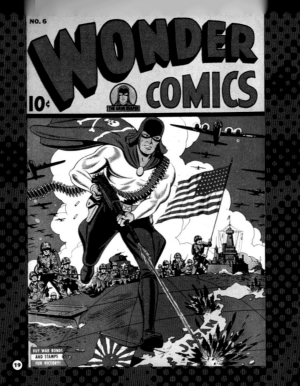

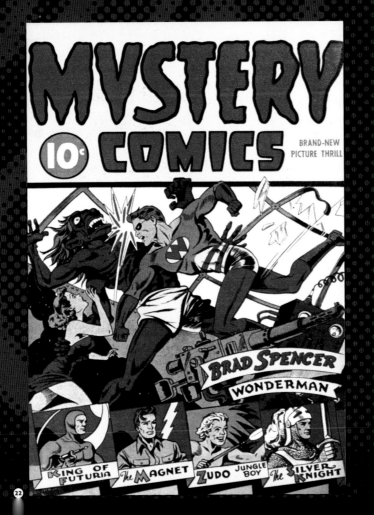

Gus Ricca. An illustrator and commercial artist, Gasparo "Gus" Ricca went to work for the Harry "A" Chesler shop about 1940. He drew interior stories for comics published by both Street & Smith and Fawcett. From 1944 to 1946, he served as art director for Chesler's new Dynamic Comics line. It was in this capacity that Ricca created a series of striking, strange, and often morbid covers for titles such as *Scoop*, *Punch*, and *Dynamic*. His work inside comic books, never anywhere near as interesting as his flamboyant covers, was last seen in the early 1950s. Little is known of his life.

⑤

②

㉖

㉔ •
PUNCH COMICS #12
January 1945
Gus Ricca

㉕ •
PUNCH COMICS #9
July 1944
Gus Ricca

㉖ •
SCOOP COMICS #8
1945
Gus Ricca

27 •
PUNCH COMICS #13
1945
Gus Ricca

28 •
DYNAMIC COMICS #18
April 1946
Gus Ricca
One of the several strange
covers Ricca drew for the Chesler
magazines in the middle 1940s.

PRIZE COMICS #8
January 1941
Gus Ricca
Ricca's version of the
Green Lama and probably
his first cover.

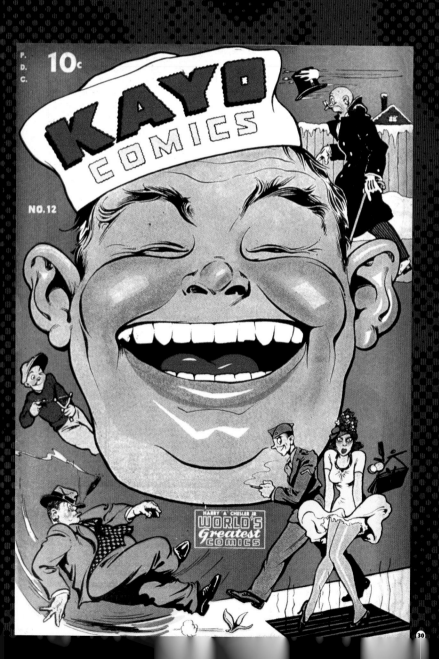

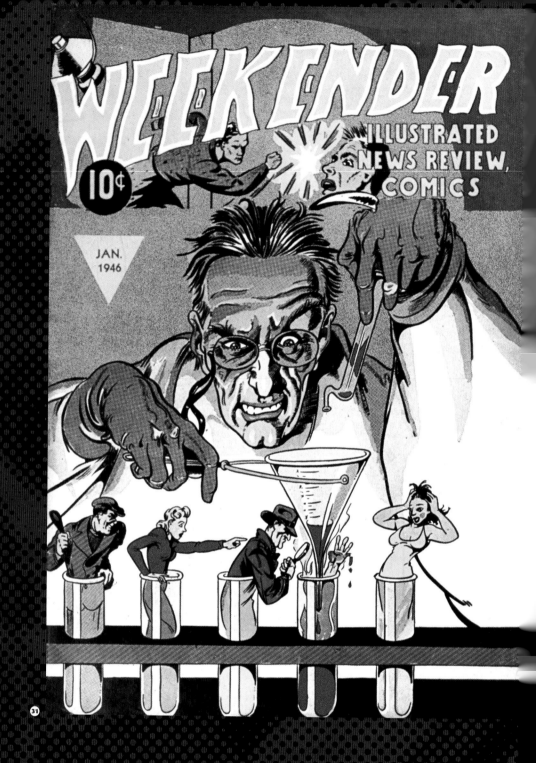

30 •
KAYO COMICS #12
1945
Gus Ricca
The only issue.

31 •
WEEKENDER
January 1945
Gus Ricca
A Canadian re-use of Ricca's
cover for *Dynamic* #11.

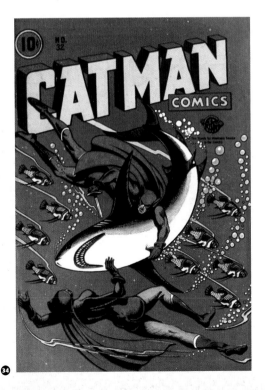

L.B. Cole. Before entering the comic book field in the early 1940s, Leonard B. Cole had worked as art director for a lithography outfit, and his specialty was designing liquor labels and cigar bands. Many of his covers were as bright and compelling as his product labels. In his early work, he always used basic, flat colors and produced what he called "poster color covers."

In an interview late in his life, Cole estimated that he'd drawn something like 1,500 covers. He drew everything from superheroes to funny animals to jungle girls, but his favorite subject matter was science fiction and he would slip rocket ships and ray guns onto magazines such as *Captain Flight* and *Contact Comics*, which were supposed to be devoted to contemporary aviation.

An enterprising fellow, Cole also published comic books. After leaving the field, he published a *Field and Stream* sort of magazine called *World Rod & Gun*. He painted some very realistic covers for that.

35 ••
Contact Comics #12
May 1946
L.B. Cole

36 ••
4 Most Boys #39
March 1950
L.B. Cole

37 ••
Captain Flight #11
February-March 1947
L.B. Cole
Cole did much of his most
striking work in the years
immediately after the end of
World War II.

38 ••
BLUE BOLT #110
August 1950
L.B. Cole

39 ••
BLUE BOLT #105
April-May 1950
L.B. Cole

A Million Laffs

Although superhumans dominated the newsstands from the late 1930s through the middle 1940s, a great many intentionally funny comic books were published during those same years. All sorts of amusing stuff was available, from relatively sophisticated satire through knockabout burlesque to the kind of bunny-rabbit whimsy guaranteed to produce giggles among the kindergarten set.

The 1940s especially was a period when publishers sought to expand their audience in both directions, luring older readers with topics such as true crime and sexy women and enticing younger readers, and their parents, with more wholesome fare. Most of the titles aimed at tots were humorous, and many of them featured animals.

The king of animals was Walt Disney and his animated cartoon characters had begun appearing on the magazine racks in the middle 1930s. *Mickey Mouse Magazine* was introduced in the summer of 1935. It was not exactly a real comic book, mixing text stories, puzzles, jokes, and a few pages of funnies. By 1940, five pages of Disney reprints, including *Mickey Mouse* newspaper dailies and, usually, a *Donald Duck* Sunday page, were to be found.

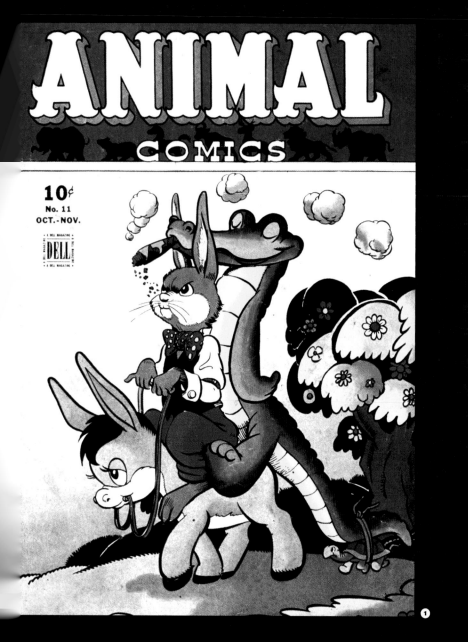

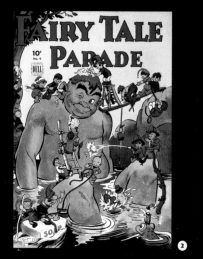

Walt Disney's Comics & Stories, in regular comic book format, replaced Mickey's mag in the autumn of 1940. Originally, the new magazine was made up almost entirely of reprints—Floyd Gottfredson's splendid mock-adventure *Mickey* dailies, Al Taliafero's funny gag-a-day *Donald Duck* strips and various Sundays, including the *Silly Symphony* pages. Then, in 1943 a change was made, and the lead story in the magazine became an original adventure of Donald. The artist and writer was a former gag cartoonist, former animator named Carl Barks. For the next twenty-five years, he served as "a sharecropper on the Disney plantation," writing and drawing the *Duck* yarn in just about every issue of *WDC&S*. Barks also turned out most of the full-length *Donald Duck* comic books and those about his creation, *Uncle Scrooge.*

In all those years, because of studio policy, Barks' name never once appeared on his work. Yet, because of the quality and individuality of what he did, he gradually became one of the best known and most admired cartoonists in the world. Allowed a much wider range than most Disney artists, Barks could say more and make fun of more things. In the full-length books, he created graphic novels that were rich with adventure, social satire, and some of the best cartoon storytelling to be found anywhere.

From the very start, Donald Duck was definitely the designated star of the new magazine. He appeared, with and without his trio of nephews, on all but two of the first hundred covers. Mickey finally showed up for the first time on the cover of #33 (June

1943), and even then he was in Donald's company. Many of the 1940s *WDC&S* covers were drawn by Walt Kelly. Later on Barks took over.

After introducing the Disney titles, Dell Publishing went on to license the Warner Brothers animated cartoon characters. The first issue of *Looney Tunes and Merry Melodies* showed up on the stands late in 1941 with individual stories devoted to Porky Pig, Elmer Fudd, and Bugs Bunny. The artwork was produced on both coasts in the early days of the magazine. Chase Craig and Roger Armstrong were based in Southern California. Kelly had returned to Manhattan after toiling at the Disney studios. *Looney Tunes* gave space to his *Kandi the Cave Kid* and other Warner characters such as Chester Turtle, Ringy Roonga, and Charlie Carrot, one of the few vegetables ever to star in a comic book feature of his own.

Andy Panda, a product of the Walter Lantz animation studios, showed up in #61 of *The Funnies* (October 1941) while the magazine was still playing host to serious characters such as Captain Midnight, Phantasmo, and Philo Vance. With the sixty-fifth issue, the title was changed to *New Funnies* and started mixing Lantz characters with comedy and fantasy characters from other sources. In addition to Andy, there were Oswald the Rabbit, Woody Woodpecker, and Li'l Eightball. From the estate of Johnny Gruelle came both *Raggedy Ann* and *Mr. Twee Deedle*.

Whitman-Dell continued its assault on the kid market with more funny creatures. The bimonthly *Animal Comics*, edited by Oskar Lebeck, commenced late

❸

4 •

GIGGLE COMICS #39

March 1947

Dan Gordon

Although he had no super powers, Super Katt had a strong desire to do good. Quite probably, he was the only costumed crime fighter to wear a baby bonnet.

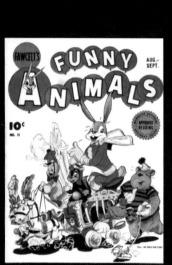

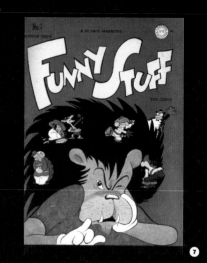

5 •

FUNNY ANIMALS #31

August-September 1944

Chad Grothkopf

The lapin member of the Marvel Family.

6 •

HI-JINX #1

July-August 1947

Dan Gordon

One of the oddest notions of the era—or any era, for that matter—was *Hi-Jinx*, filled with stories about teenage animals.

7 •

FUNNY STUFF #7

Winter 1945

Sheldon Mayer

Mayer edited this title, provided covers, and, on one occasion, drew the whole issue.

8 •

COO COO COMICS #17

May 1945

Victor E. Pazmino

The magazine was devoted mostly to funny animals. Chief among them was Supermouse, who derived his powers from eating Super-Cheese.

in 1941. This was where Walt Kelly's *Pogo* began his long and successful career. Though the original star of the magazine was meant to be Howard Garis' venerable rabbit gentleman Uncle Wiggily, Pogo and his swampland associates eventually pushed him into a secondary position. Initially, Pogo was just a spear carrier, handicapped, as Kelly later pointed out, because he "looked just like a possum. As time went on, this condition was remedied, and Pogo took on a lead role."

Kelly also contributed nineteen of *Animal Comics'* thirty covers. On several occasions, he depicted a somewhat uneasy Uncle Wiggily interfacing with his brash, cigar-smoking alligator. The first comic book filled with nothing but Pogo came along in the spring of 1946, entitled *Albert the Alligator & Pogo Possum*. By 1949, a *Pogo Possum* magazine was being issued on a fairly regular basis, and a *Pogo* newspaper strip was begun that same year.

Our Gang Comics, *Raggedy Ann and Andy*, and *Fairy Tale Parade* all arrived in 1942, offering mixed bags of animal and human characters. In *Our Gang*, Walt Kelly drew his version of the adventures of the kids from the MGM comedy shorts, blending melodrama and slapstick. Also adapted from MGM properties were Tom & Jerry, Benny Burro, and Barney Bear. Carl Barks took over Benny and eventually teamed the burro with the bear. Kelly usually drew about half of every issue of the fairy-tale book and, entirely by himself, produced the contents of occasional titles such as *Christmas with Mother Goose*.

Marvel's earliest funny-animal title was *Krazy Komics*, introduced in the summer of 1942. In that one, editor Vince Fago and a staff that included Kin Platt, George Klein, Dave Gantz, Al Jaffee, and a youthful Stan Lee invented a crew of animated cartoon-type characters. These included Posty Pelican, Toughy Tomcat & Chester Chipmunk, and Jaffee's Silly Seal & Ziggy Pig. There was also an odd strip called *The Creeper & Homer*, featuring a mysterious cloaked villain and a not very astute rabbit. It managed now and then to get most of the magazine's artists and writers into the stories, and on one occasion publisher Martin Goodman himself appeared to complain—"Ah, woe is me! Krazy Komics is 14 months late, and my laundry hasn't come back from Stan Lee's." Later in the year, *Terry Toons*, adapted from Paul Terry's lackluster movie cartoons, was added to the Marvel list. And in the fall of 1944, Super Rabbit, a character who'd first shown up in *Comedy Comics*, was given a book of his own.

Originally Fawcett announced that its entry in the animation derby would be called *Animal Funny Stories*, but when the magazine finally appeared toward the end of 1942, the title was the somewhat catchier *Fawcett's Funny Animals*. This being their first venture away from straight heroes, they went to someone with experience in the animated-cartoon field to help them turn out their new comic book. The Chicago-born Chad Grothkopf was in this late twenties at the time and had worked in California for Disney.

Chad had come east in 1938, when NBC had asked him to work on the first cartoon show for the network's fledgling animation operation.

Getting together with Fawcett executive Ralph Daigh, Chad came up with a batch of new characters. These included Sherlock Monk, Billy the Kid—a goat cowboy—and Willie the Worm. The leading character was yet another member of the Marvel Family—Hoppy the Marvel Bunny. Like Captain Marvel, he had but to exclaim, "Shazam!" to turn into a red-clad superhero. The original captain appeared on the cover of the first issue along with Hoppy and the rest of the cast.

The All-American branch, under the editorship of Sheldon Mayer, produced DC's first funny-animal title. *Funny Stuff*, a quarterly, commenced in the summer of 1944. Mayer drew J. Rufus Lion, an animal kingdom version of the boastful windbag Major Hoople. The Three Mouseketeers, Blackie Bear, and Bulldog Drumhead were also in the troop. One of the more interesting characters was McSnurtle the Turtle, alias the Terrific Whatzit. This was a parody of the

Flash and offered McSnurtle in a miniature Flash costume, winged helmet and all. Martine Naydell, who drew it, was also drawing the serious Flash at the time.

DC turned to movie-cartoon characters in 1945 with *Real Screen Comics*. This starred the Fox and Crow, a team that had been appearing in a series of Columbia Pictures shorts. The Fox was the perennial patsy, the Crow was the eternal con man who fooled, flimflammed, hoodwinked, and otherwise took advantage of him. "Whit Ellsworth came out looking

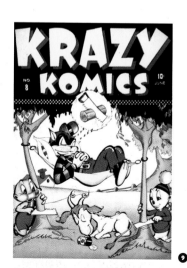

❾ ••
KRAZY KOMICS #8
June 1943
Unknown
The Marvel approach to funny animals. That's the splendidly named Ziggy Pig manning one of the saws.

❿ ••
JOKER COMICS #2
June 1942
Unknown
The magazine that introduced both Basil Wolverton's *Powerhouse Pepper* and Al Jaffee's *Squatcar Squad* to the world.

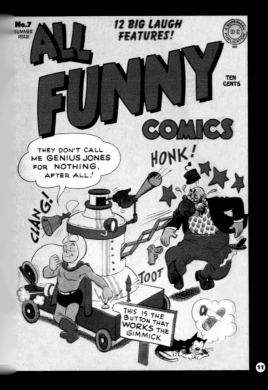

13 •

JINGLE JANGLE COMICS #6
December 1942
George Carlson
Another comic book brought
to you by the folks who were
behind *Famous Funnies*.

14 •

ALL HUMOR COMICS #13
Spring 1949
Bart Tumey
Like Jack Cole, Tumey drew
both serious and comedy
features. He even did a stretch
ghosting Jack Cole's *Plastic Man*.

15 •

ALL HUMOR COMICS #2
Summer 1946
Jack Cole
Brains, brawn, and Jack Cole
could not make *Odd Jobs, Inc.*, a hit.

THE EXTRA SALTY SAILOR AND THE FLAT-
FOOTED DRAGON, BINGO'S FROLICS IN
FAIRYTALE LAND, FROG POND FERRY,
HORTENSE — THE LOVABLE BRAT,
BOTTLENECK & WIDGET, PIEFACE PRINCE,
JOLLY-O AND SUSIE SPRING.

13

14

15

16

17

16 •
JINGLE JANGLE COMICS #15
June 1944
Larz Bourne
Artist Bourne also worked
in animation.

17 •

SPARKY WATTS #2
1943
Creig Flessel
Boody Rogers' sparsely
syndicated newspaper strip
became much more successful
when reprinted.

for a cartoon subject," explained animator James F. Davis. "The only thing available was Columbia." Davis, in addition to working as an animator, was heading up the West Coast branch of the Ben Sangor art shop. Based in New York, Sangor was in partnership with publisher Fred Iger. Eventually they called themselves the American Comics Group and published a string of comic books, but the shop also turned out great quantities of artwork and packaged comic books for other publishers.

The Sangor specialty was funny animals, and in Hollywood Davis, who took over the drawing of the Fox and Crow in 1948, rode herd over a bunch of moonlighting movie animators and writers. "Well, there were 65 of us working on those things at one time," he once recalled, "and we used to send back sheets of Strathmore two-feet high every month." Eventually DC added other animal titles, such as *Funny Folks*, and converted hero comics like *Leading Comics*. This latter magazine featured a character with the catchy name of Peter Porkchops.

From Sangor also came the contents of the Pines animated comics—*Barnyard*, *Happy*, *Goofy*, and *Coo Coo*. In *Coo Coo Comics*, readers found the one and only Supermouse, whose "great powers, you know, stem from his SUPERCHEESE." Under the ACG banner were *Ha Ha Comics* and *Giggle Comics*. Superkatt was the star of *Giggle*. He wore a hero costume that consisted of a baby bonnet, a bow tie, and a diaper and had a mutt dog for a sidekick. Dan Gordon, a former animator working in New York, was the creator of this

particular epic. An inventive artist with an appealing style, Gordon drew dozens of funny animal covers in the 1940s, including all eight for the short-lived *Hi-Jinx*. This title was devoted entirely to the antics of teenage animal characters.

Many publishers also tried humor with characters that were human, more or less. In 1942, Marvel launched *Joker Comics*. Headlining it was Basil Wolverton's Powerhouse Pepper, the only bald superhero of his day. Besides being hairless, Powerhouse didn't have a superman suit. He usually combated evil wearing a striped turtleneck sweater, slacks, and heavy work shoes.

Although *Powerhouse Pepper* owed a bit to newspaper strips such as *Smokey Stover* and movies like Olsen and Johnson's *Hellzapoppin*, it was still 99 percent pure Wolverton—high-class and lowbrow, inventive and audacious, very much in tune with the baggy-pants burlesque comedy that flourished in this country during World War II. Before Powerhouse was many issues old, Wolverton had given way to his compulsive fascination with alliteration and reached the point where he couldn't even sign his name straight. Instead, he would use "by Basil Baboonbrain Wolverton," "by Basil Weirdrdwit Wolverton," "by Basil Bucketbeak Wolverton," etc.

He was equally fond of internal rhyme and his dialogue as well as numerous signs and posters that cluttered almost every inch of wall (and often floor and ceiling) space was full of the stuff. "Zounds! Your snappers are as sound as a hound's," one of the physicians giving Powerhouse his Army physical observes. The three medical fellows involved in this chore are named Dr. Ash Gash, Dr. Bill Drill, and Dr. Jack Hack. Our hero is rejected because of his head. "You're out, sport, because it's hopeless to hang a helmet on a head like yours!" "Isn't my bean clean?" inquires the crestfallen Powerhouse. "It's too lean, if you know what I mean! See? A helmet teeters over your cheaters, and there's no way to clap a strap under your map!" "Fap! I must look like a sap!"

Ending up in Egypt in this episode—sign in the sand: Will Sara wear a Sahara tiara?—Powerhouse encounters a reanimated mummy and escorts him back to America. After viewing the joys of modern civilization, which include a visit to a restaurant named simply Crude Food, wherein are offered such delights as blue blackbirds broiled in brown bovine

butter and buzz bugs basted in bilge water, the mummy decided to return to his case. In addition to the bald hero, Joker also showcased Jaffee's *Squat Car Squad* as well as *Snoopy and Dr. Nutzy*, *Tessie the Typist*, and an assortment of other funny fillers.

Although the incomparable Wolverton's work was seen *inside* a variety of comic books—ranging from *Silver Streak Comics* to *Comic Comics*—he did only a few covers. This was probably because, unlike most of his comic book contemporaries, he dwelled not in the vicinity of New York City but in the far-off Pacific Northwest.

DC brought out its first all funny human title in 1943, calling it, aptly enough, *All Funny Comics*. A quarterly, it boasted that its sixty-four pages contained "12 Big Laugh Features!" Some of the characters, such as the impecunious private eye Penniless Palmer and the costumed human encyclopedia Genius Jones (created by SF author Alfred Bester and cartoonist Stan Kaye), had been borrowed from other DC titles. Among the brand new characters were Two-Gun Percy, Hamilton & Egbert, and a teenager named Buzzy. Several of the cartoonists recruited for the humor project were well beyond draft age. Among the newspaper and magazine veterans, some of whom had been turning out funny stuff since before the World War I, were Tom McNamara, Jack Farr, Jack Callahan, Jimmy Thompson, Ray McGill, Paul Fung, and George Storm.

The Quality line also attempted a comedy title, but waited until early 1946 to start *All Humor Comics*. An uninspired venture, despite early contributions

❶❺ •
MUTT & JEFF #6
Fall 1942
Sheldon Mayer
Publisher M.C. Gaines was long fascinated with Bud Fisher's characters, reprinting their newspaper strips in various magazines and finally introducing a whole comic book devoted to them. The strips recycled in the magazine were mostly ones ghosted by the dependable Al Smith.

by the inventive Jack Cole, it lasted for seventeen issues before expiring in the winter of 1949. The leading character for most of the run was Bart Tumey's Kelly Poole, a roughneck, derby-wearing Moon Mullins surrogate.

A strange and fleeting entry was *Milt Gross Funnies*. Written, drawn, and apparently published by newspaper veteran Milt Gross, it surfaced just twice in 1947. In the 1920s and 1930s, Gross had been a newspaper success with features such as *Nize Baby*, which was both a column and a comic strip, *Banana Oil*, *Count Screwloose*, *Dave's Delicatessen*, and *That's My Pop!* He drew in a loose, bold, nervous style, most of his characters were cross-eyed, and he made use in his early work of the Jewish dialect he'd heard growing up in the Bronx. Gross also produced books, including a graphic novel called *He Done Her Wrong*—"Not a word in it. No music, too." By the early 1940s, he'd left newspapers and was residing in Hollywood. He provided artwork for such films as the Bing Crosby-Betty Hutton musical *Here Come The Waves* and the Ginger Rogers comedy *Roxie Hart*. Later in the decade, he started contributing fillers for comic books like *Picture News*, *Giggle*, and *Hi-Jinx*. The two issues of his own magazine revived old favorites *That's My Pop!*, *Count Screwloose*, and *Banana Oil* among others. An eccentric one-of-a-kind cartoonist, Gross never succeeded in finding a comfortable niche in the comic books of the period.

Early in 1942, Famous Funnies, Inc., introduced *Jingle Jangle Comics*, a title that provided a mix of human and funny animal features. Steve Douglas was

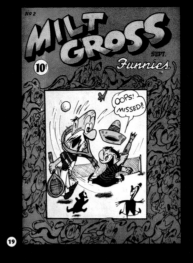

19 •
MILT GROSS FUNNIES #2
September 1947
Milt Gross
Once a nationally syndicated comic-strip artist, Gross did his last professional work in 1940s comic books.

20 •
FAT AND SLAT #2
Fall 1947
Ed Wheelan
The inventive Wheelan was able to convert two characters from his *Minute Movies*— a newspaper strip in the 1920s and 1930s and a comic book feature in the 1940s— into rivals of Mutt & Jeff.

the editor and George Carlson the star cartoonist. A veteran children's book illustrator and puzzlemaker, Carlson was in his middle fifties by the time he finally ventured into comic books. He'd had a varied career that included creating the dust jacket painting for Margaret Mitchell's *Gone With The Wind* and ghosting the *Reg'lar Fellers* newspaper strip. Carlson had been kicking around the *Jingle Jangle* notion for several years, having already tried it as a children's book and, unsuccessfully, a newspaper Sunday page. Each issue of the magazine included two of his features—*Jingle Jangle Tales* and *The Pie-Face Prince*.

Carlson was a one-man band of a cartoonist who did scripting, pencilling, inking—the works. For his efforts he eventually earned twenty-five dollars a page for the dozen pages of material he turned out for each issue. His tales mixed burlesque, fantasy, and word play with his individualistic brand of non-sense. He brought a sophisticated approach to fairy tales, turning out multilevel material in which the visual and the verbal elements worked together. Quite obviously Carlson was amusing himself first and foremost.

Among the characters who did turns in Carlson's *Jingle Jangle Tales* were the Youthful Yodeler, who lived on a newly painted mountain and sold all kinds of weath-er by the yard; the Half-Champion Archer, who wasn't a full-time champ because he never hit the king's special Tuesday target; the Very Horseless Jockey, who became rich from a flavored-snowball business and then set out, via a steamed-up steam engine, to buy a fine mahogany horse for himself. A fascinating vari-ety of unusual props, people, and creatures wandered through Carlson's lively, cluttered pages.

Pretzleburg, ruled over by King Hokum without noticeable help from his pie-face offspring Prince Dimwitri, was a place that brought an inspired silli-ness to the conventions of light opera. The recurrent players were Princess Panetella Murphy, who was more or less Dimwitri's sweetheart and could some-times be found dwelling in "her left-footed uncle's second-best castle;" the Raging Raja, billed as the Prince's "favorite enemy;" and the Wicked Green Witch (a longtime resident of Connecticut, Carlson was no doubt inspired by the common mispronunci-ation of Greenwich). Prince Dimwitri's interests and adventures were wide-ranging. In one issue, he set out to find the coveted Doopsniggle Prize with his corned beef-flavored cabbage plant in tow; in anoth-er he went aloft in an eighteen-carat balloon in search of a missing bass drum.

While *Jingle Jangle* appealed to children and prob-ably captivated its share of adults, too, it didn't have much appeal for the teenage audience. Fairly early in the 1940s, publishers discovered that stories about teenagers could be highly saleable. Adolescents had only recently been discovered to be a separate tribe. Publishers, film producers, and other entrepreneurs looked at adolescents and saw a large segment of the population whose antics could be exploited for entertainment purposes and who had money of their own to spend.

22 ·
COOKIE #8
August-September 1947
Dan Gordon
A much more slapstick version
of teen life was presented in the
Cookie stories. Possibly because
artist Gordon had worked many
years in animation.

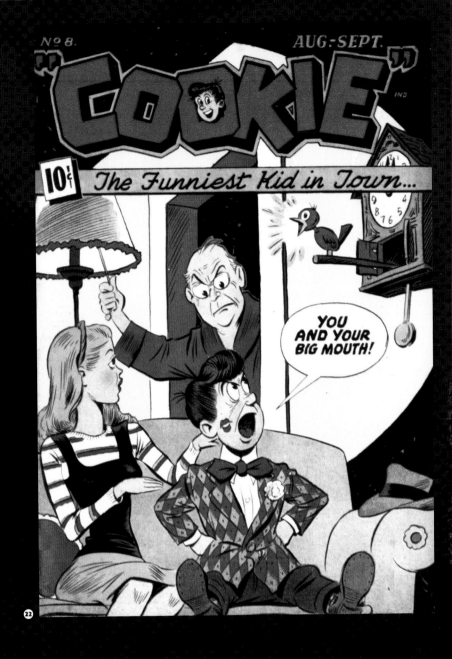

21 ·
COOKIE #20
August-September 1949
Dan Gordon

23 ·
COOKIE #9
October-November 1947
Dan Gordon

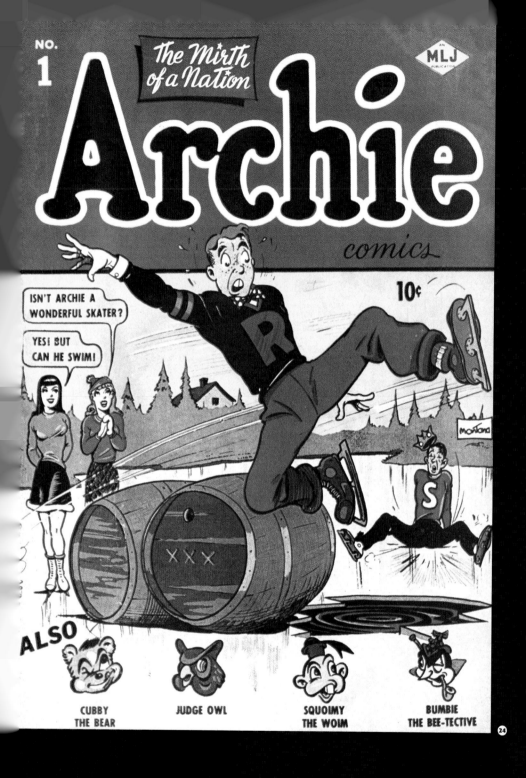

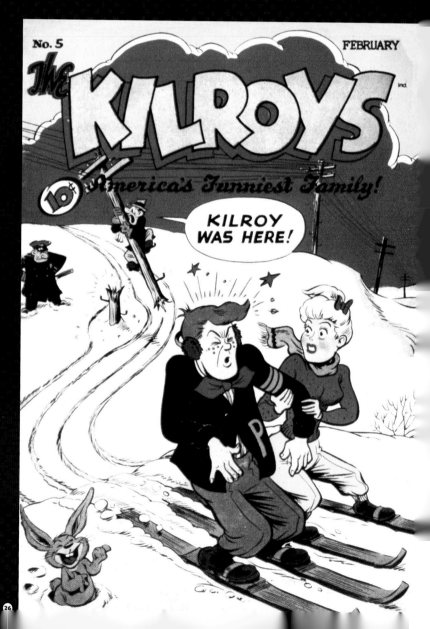

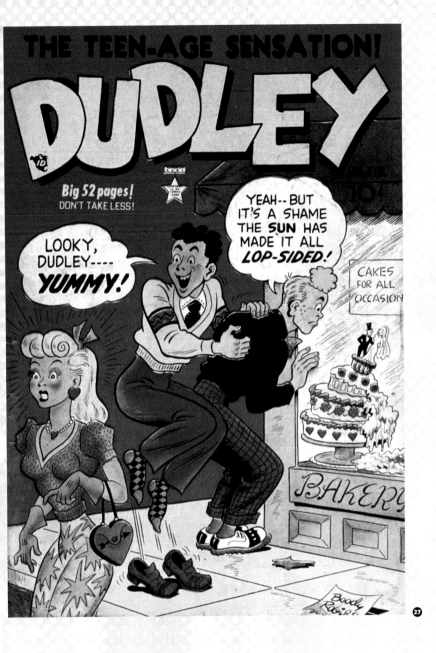

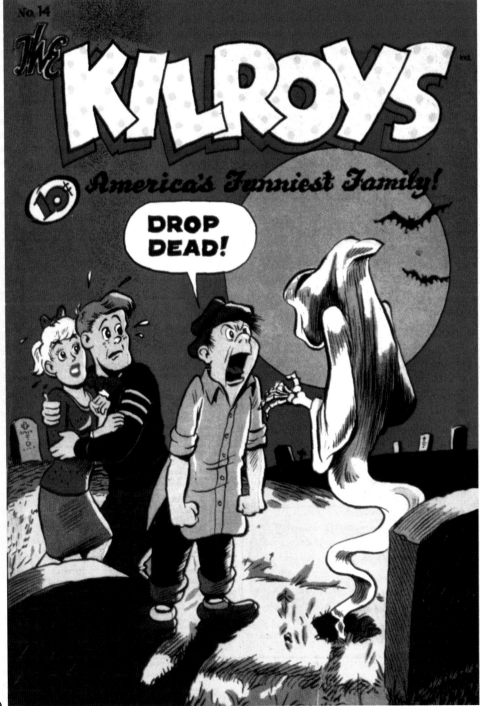

27 •

DUDLEY #2
January-February 1950
Boody Rogers
Rogers had first drawn for comic books in 1929, when he contributed to *The Funnies*.

28 •

THE KILROYS #14
November 1949
Dan Gordon

29 •

WOW COMICS #63
February 1948
Unknown
As the teenage craze blossomed, Fawcett tossed out Mary Marvel and replaced her with Archie surrogate Ozzie.

30 •
KEEN TEENS #2
1946
Creig Flessel
A semi-comic book that
contained strips reprints,
original comics, articles,
and photos of then-film-stars
such as Van Johnson.

31 •
JOE COLLEGE COMICS #1
Fall 1949
David Berg
Apparently college kids
didn't appeal to fans of teen
characters, and this title
lasted but one more issue.

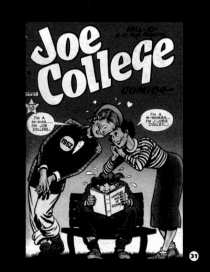

High-school kids began to get serious public notice in the 1930s, when swing music and the jitterbug dance craze helped put them on the map. Suddenly, the high-energy antics of high-school boys and girls were noted by newspapers, magazines, and newsreels. This caught the attention not only of teenagers and their often perplexed parents, but also of younger children who couldn't wait to be teenagers themselves.

Henry Aldrich, the well-meaning but bumbling teen who was the prime inspiration for the early comic book high schoolers, first appeared in 1938 in Clifford Goldsmith's Broadway play *What A Life*. Henry and his pal Homer soon made the leap to radio and then to movies. Not to be outdone, MGM came up with a teenager of their own in the person of Andy Hardy. Preoccupied with girls, cars, and school, Henry and Andy saw no reason why they shouldn't have all the rights and perks of adulthood, especially since they'd be grown up any day now. Their elaborate schemes and dreams of glory led them into all sorts of unforeseen complications and caused considerable anxiety for their devoted but puzzled parents.

MLJ was the first comic book company to be seriously influenced by the newly emergent American teenager. Beginning in 1941, they started adding characters to titles that had heretofore contained nothing but superhumans, masked marvels, and assorted violent vigilantes. MLJ's most successful kid star was Bob Montana's Archie, who changed not just the company's fortunes but its very name as well.

Archie arrived in *Pep Comics* #22 and *Jackpot Comics* #4, previously citadels of costumed crimefighters, including the Shield, Hangman, Steel Sterling, and Mr. Justice. The red-haired, freckled Riverside High student was accompanied by his wholesome blonde girlfriend, Betty, and his deceptively dimwitted pal, Jughead. The dark-haired Veronica came slinking into Archie's life a few months later. This version of teen life was one that a great many young readers took to, and the character's star began to rise. The first issue of Archie's own magazine came out in the fall of 1942, and by late 1947, he'd nudged all the serious heroes out of *Pep*. Bob Montana had left the Archie comic books for the service and then the new *Archie* comic strip. Among the many artists who carried on were Harry Sahle, Al Fagaly, and Dan DeCarlo.

The Quality Comics Group's most successful teenager showed up late in 1944 in, of all places, *Police Comics*. Beginning with #37, sexy, chestnut-haired Candy rubbed shoulders with Plastic Man, the Spirit, and the Human Bomb. She was the creation of Harry Shale, who'd recently departed from the Archie stable. Candy was much like the energetic young ladies featured on *A Date With Judy*, *Meet Corliss Archer*, and similar popular radio shows. Both Judy and Corliss, by the way, eventually got comic books of their own. Candy won her own comic in the summer of 1947 and enjoyed a run of sixty-four issues.

DC gave George Storm's *Buzzy* a magazine in 1944 and later added teen titles such as *Leave It To Binky*. The American Comics Group brought additional slapstick

to the teen formula with *Cookie*, another invention of Dan Gordon. Cookie had the usual cast—an irascible businessman father, an understanding mom, a beautiful blonde girlfriend named Angelpuss, a slang-spouting pal name of Jitterbuck, and a handsome, conniving rival called Zoot. Gordon's stories differed from the standard adolescent fare in that they were full of violent pratfalls and lowbrow jokes and gags involving outrageous props. They were much more like the animated cartoons he'd once concocted.

Teen titles continued to proliferate into the later 1940s and were one of the factors that contributed to the temporary demise of superheroes. Kathy, Ozzie, Ginger, Jeanie, Junior, Mitzi, Patsy Walker, and even Henry Aldrich, along with dozens of others, were to be found on the roster of just about every comic book publisher.

❸❷ •
CALLING ALL GIRLS #1
January 1946
A sedate mix of comics
and articles produced by
Parents Magazine, **who also offered**
the equally dull *Calling All Boys*.

As World War II spread across Europe in the late 1930s, comic books began to take notice. The United States didn't officially enter the War until December of 1941, after the Japanese attack on Pearl Harbor. But in the anxious years leading up to that event, as war jitters increased, the concerns of Americans—especially kid readers—as Hitler's war devastated Europe were frequently reflected in the magazines and on their covers.

References to soldiers and battles started showing up in various stories and early heroes, most notably Superman himself, were seen battling dictators and warmongers—often, however, in mythical countries and kingdoms. Finally in the spring of 1940 an entire comic book devoted to war hit the stands. Called simply and directly *War Comics*, it was published by Dell and offered both fictional and fact-based combat yarns. Previously Dell had limited itself pretty much to polite reprint titles such as *Popular Comics*, *The Funnies*, and *Walt Disney's Comics and Stories*. The new magazine, with its cover logo showing the blood-red letters W, A, and R exploding, was something of a departure. The contents were not especially bloody, with most of the violence involving explosions and aerial warfare rather than hand-to-hand combat.

War employed artist Alden McWilliams, one of the best planes, ships, and weapons experts in comics at the time, to handle its nonfiction—accounts of the Scapa Flow and Graf Spee incidents, etc. Among the fictional characters were two separate war correspondents, Scoop Mason and Danny Dash, as well as a daredevil Navy pilot nicknamed the Sky Hawk—he was already unofficially fighting the Japanese in 1940—and a fellow called the Peace Raider, who fought a freelance seagoing war against "the warmongers of the world." For some reason, there was also a superhero named Greg Gilday, who specialized in handling threats to national security such as invaders from Mars. The fourth issue introduced two chaps who dressed in skintight, hooded black outfits to parachute into enemy territory and act like costumed commandos. Initially known as Black Wings, they later did business as Night Devils.

Apparently the public wasn't ready for a comic book totally focused on war, and *War* only appeared eight times in its three years of existence. Dell also produced a one-shot, *USA Is Ready*, in 1941. It was a boastful comic about how well-prepared America was for war. After the Axis powers took up the challenge, Dell introduced *War Heroes* and *War Stories*.

Street & Smith, who'd been in publishing since before the Civil War, took notice of the World War II in the spring of 1941. They introduced a quarterly entitled *Army and Navy Comics*, aimed not only at kids but at the multitude of young men who, under the new draft law, were being inducted into the service. The magazine, calling itself "every Army camp's favorite," took a much lighter approach than *War Comics* and aimed chiefly to entertain. In 1942, Street & Smith published a one-shot called *Remember Pearl Harbor*. This mix of text and comics featured nonfiction stories extolling the superior training and courage of American servicemen. One important point the magazine made was that while the enemy stressed "blind obedience" in its fighting men, the United States favored teamwork—"it has WON our other WARS."

In the nonwar comic books, there had also been a growing preoccupation with the subject. At first it was a sort of generic war that was depicted, with no specific references to the Axis armies. The cover of *Action Comics* #10, for example, featured Superman smashing what looked to be a warplane, and the cover of the next issue depicts a conflict between a ship and a submarine. On *Action* #17, Superman is lifting up a

tank in a battlefield setting, on #19 he's ripping apart a canon, and on #21 he can be seen attacking a U-boat. For the next several months, the Man of Steel limited himself to domestic crimes. Then, on the cover of #31 (December 1940), he rescued a political prisoner from a firing squad. On his own

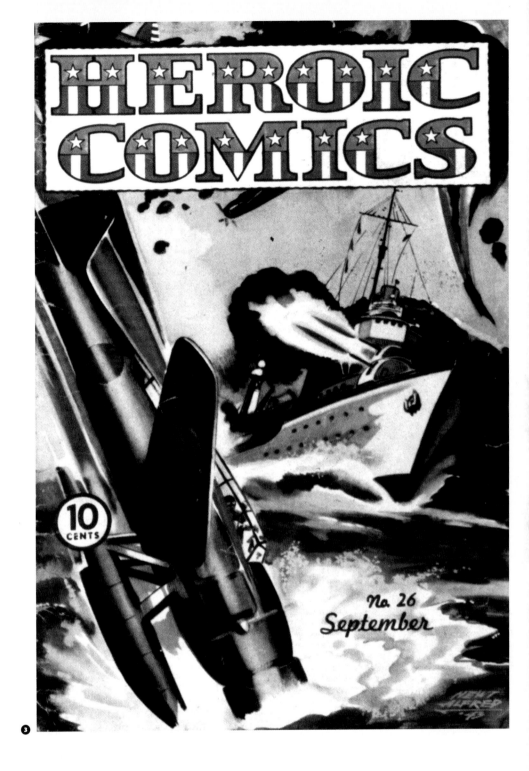

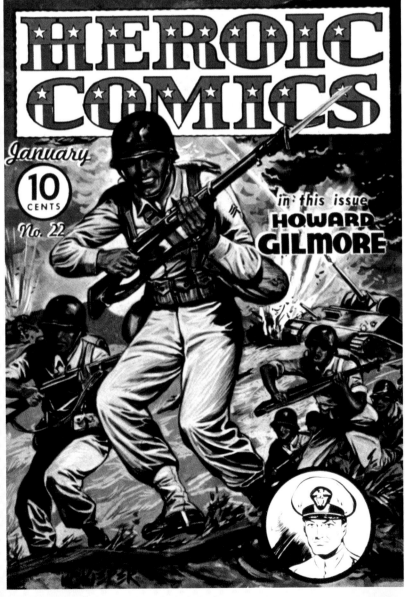

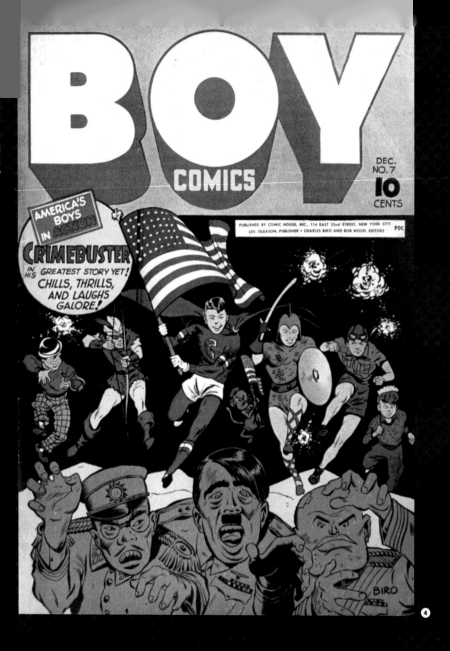

BOY COMICS #7
December 1942
Charles Biro (and Norman Maurer)
Though the magazine's
boy heroes were too young for
the armed forces, they
were old enough to go after
the Axis powers.

AMERICA'S BEST COMICS #10
July 1944
Alex Schomburg
With Allied flags waving,
Doc Strange, the Black Terror,
the American Eagle, and
Pyroman tromp on the banners
of the Axis.

6 ..

STARS AND STRIPES COMICS #2
May 1941
Paul Gustavson
The characters in the new,
patriotically titled magazine,
all from *Amazing-Man Comics*,
stage a parade.

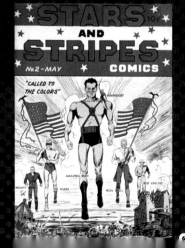

8 ··
BIG 3 #3
May 1941
Edd Ashe
A trio of Fox superheroes
pledges allegiance to the flag.

9 ··
BIG 3 #7
January 1942
Ramona Patenaude
With V-Man replacing Samson,
the trio takes to the battlefield.

7 ···
MASTER COMICS #21
December 1941
Mac Raboy
Even Hitler, according to
Master Comics, had a superhero
on his staff. Here Captain
Nazi sneers at Captain Marvel
and Bulletman in his best
Eric Von Stroheim manner.

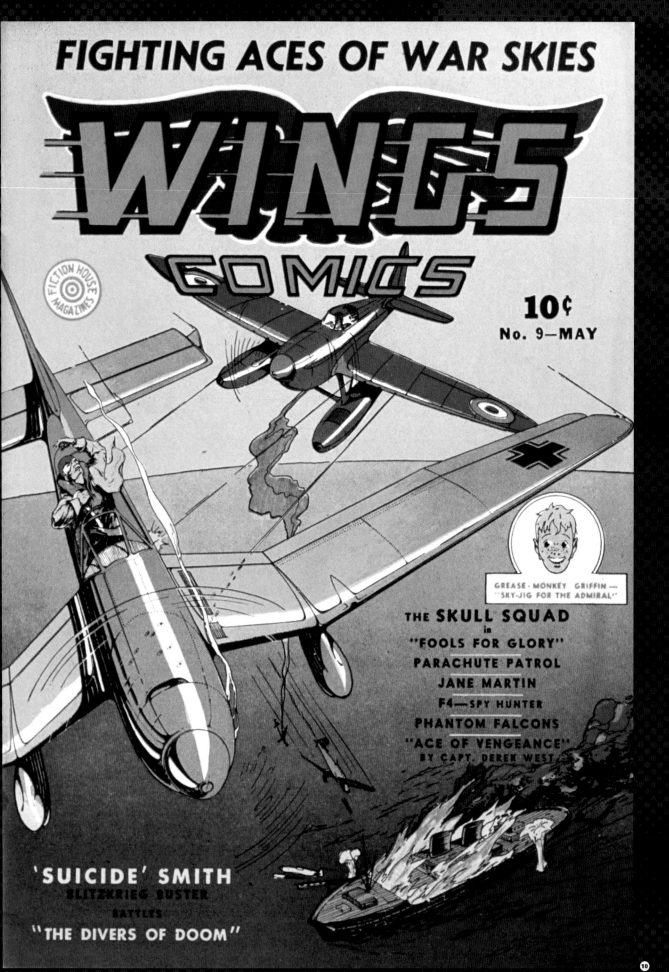

⑫ •
POPULAR COMICS #46
December 1939
Alden McWilliams
Generic war scenes were
already appearing by the end
of the 1930s.

⑬ ••
HEROIC COMICS #2
October 1940
Bill Everett
Partially liquefied, Hydroman
is about to knock an Asian
invader out of the sky.

⑭ •
CRACKAJACK FUNNIES #24
June 1940
Alden McWilliams
Aerial warfare
was a frequent subject.

16 •

The United States Marines
1943
Creig Flessel
This could've been used as
a propaganda poster at the time.

17 • • •

Military Comics #1
August 1941
Will Eisner
Eisner, who edited this bellicose
addition to the Quality line,
was co-creator of Blackhawk.

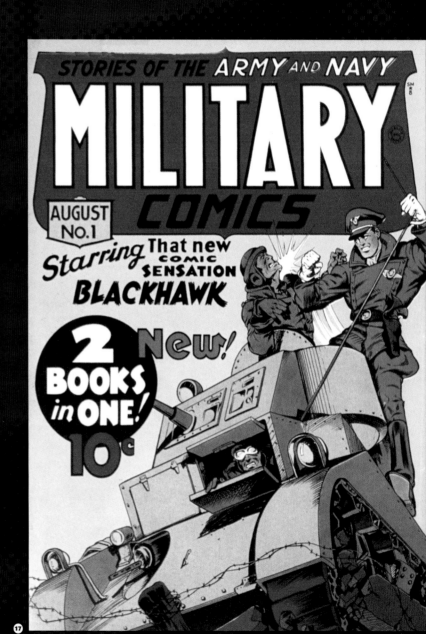

15 • •

Big Shot Comics #13
May 1941
Fred Guardineer
Captain Devildog began
active comic book duty in the
spring of 1941.

magazine he didn't engage in any war-related activities until #7, when he tackled another warplane. On the front of *Superman* #12 (September–October 1941), he's marching arm-in-arm with a sailor and a soldier, and on #13, he's saving a lifeboat full of torpedo raid survivors from being machine gunned. The machine gunners shown in Fred Ray's drawing are obviously meant to be Nazis, but the symbol on their boat was a cross and not a swastika. Once America entered the War, that policy changed at DC, and identifiable German and Japanese enemies would appear on the covers.

The first issue of *Speed Comics* in 1939 showed superhero Shock Gibson lifting up a tank on a battlefield; the cover of the second issue had him fighting warplanes, and on the third he was back on the battlefield hoisting an artillery piece over his head. Interestingly, Shock seemed to go in for war encounters similar to those indulged in by Superman, in some cases performing his feats before his more famous rival.

18 •
WAR COMICS #2
May 1941
Alden McWilliams
The first all-out war title.

19 •
WAR STORIES #8
February–April 1943
Blah
This is *War Comics* under its new name.

20 ••
EXCITING COMICS #33
June 1944
Alex Schomburg
Somewhere in Germany,
the Black Terror arrives just
in time to save his partner
Tim from a Nazi firing squad.

21 ••
THRILLING COMICS #19
August 1941
Alex Schomburg
Doc Strange battles for
Great Britain. The issue also
introduced the American
Crusader, the Fighting
Defender of Democracy.

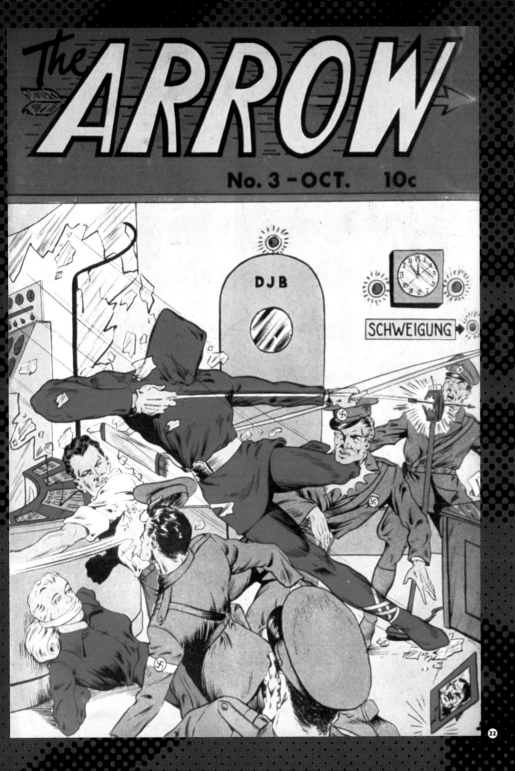

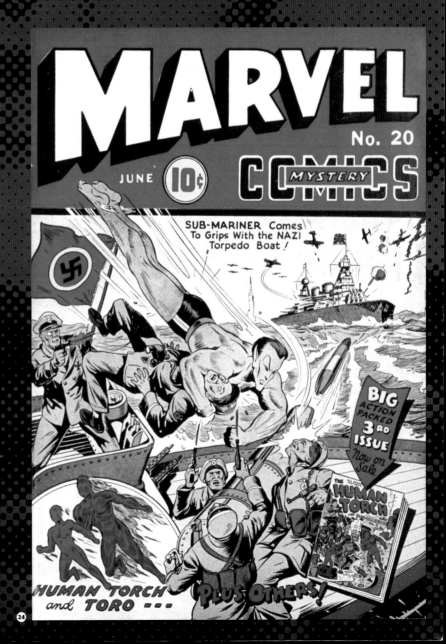

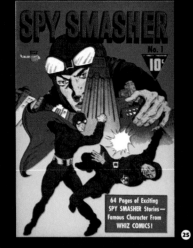

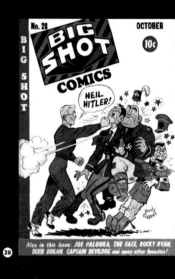

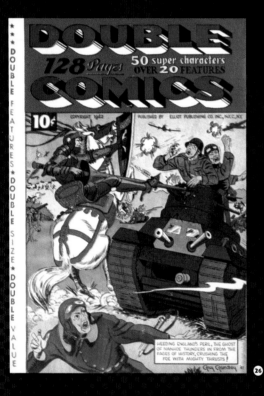

27 •

BIG SHOT COMICS #25
July 1942
Boody Rogers
Mock superman Sparky Watts
does his part. Cartoonist
Rogers went into the Army
himself about this time.

28 •

BIG SHOT COMICS #28
October 1942
Boody Rogers

29 ••

CAMP COMICS #3
April 1942
A title aimed at the GIs
who were buying their comic
books at the post exchanges.
With a pin-up girl on the
cover and contributions from
Walt Kelly, Frank Thomas,
and Ralph Carlson.

30 •

WOW COMICS #22
February 1944
Jack Binder
Mary Marvel as a USO pinup girl—
a cover that must have pleased the
Office of War Information.

25 ••

SPY SMASHER #1
Fall 1941
Charles Sultan
On a symbolic cover, *Whiz
Comics'* counter-espionage
hero slugs a lone Nazi invader.

26 ••

DOUBLE COMICS
1942
Ray Ramsey
Double slapped a new cover on a
pair of newsstand return issues
and sold them for a dime.

Many other comic book covers were offering war scenes as the 1940s got underway. *Heroic Comics* #2 showed Bill Everett's aqueous Hydroman fighting an Oriental combat pilot; *Master Comics* #7 had a C.C. Beck cover wherein Bulletman battled parachute troopers; *Thrilling Comics* #19 showed Doc Strange

COME ON, BOYS— EVERYBODY SING!

MARY MARVEL

SONG-SLIDE GIRL OF OUR FIGHTING MEN

LEADS A PUNCHING PARADE OF HEROES IN THIS ISSUE!

★

COMMANDO YANK ★ MR. SCARLET AND PINKY ★ PHANTOM EAGLE

thwarting a Nazi bombing plane in the sky over Manhattan. Even *The Funnies* used several war covers in 1940—all of them drawn by Alden McWilliams.

Beyond a doubt, Marvel was the least neutral of any of the prewar comic book publishers. They started running clearly labeled Nazis on the covers of their magazines early in 1940. The first such cover, which appeared on *Marvel Mystery Comics* #4 (February 1940), showed the Sub-Mariner tangling with the crew of a German submarine. After a succession of monsters and hooded fiends, Nazis were seen again on #10 as the Sub-Mariner this time single-handedly sunk a U-boat. The following months readers saw the Human Torch melting a swastika-emblazoned tank. Of the rest of the covers for the remainder of 1940 and all of 1941, eleven of them depicted the Torch or the Sub-Mariner, and sometimes the pair of them, mopping up dozens of Nazi troops. A Japanese soldier didn't appear until #30 (April 1942) after the attack on Pearl Harbor.

The Human Torch, along with his boy sidekick Toro, got a title of his own in the summer of 1940. The fiery team shared the new book with the Sub-Mariner, and on the cover of the first issue they can be seen devastating yet another Nazi sub. When the Sub-Mariner added his own title, early in 1941, he was depicted on the initial cover sinking a boatload of German invasion troops. The artist on most of these bellicose covers was the dependable and inventive Alex Schomburg.

As the 1930s ended, a growing patriotic fervor swept America. "Americans had dragged their patriotism out of the closet," reported *Life* in its July 22, 1940, issue, "and were wearing it in the streets as they had not done since 1918. Every musical show on Broadway featured the national anthem as a curtain-raiser or finale. Red, white and blue gallantly gleamed on lapels, umbrellas, hats and suspenders. Patriotic pins, pendants, clips and bracelets 'walked off the counters' of department and five-and-dime stores as fast as they could be stocked."

The first superpatriotic hero was the Shield. His star-spangled costume was adapted from the American flag and set the style for what the well-dressed ultra-patriotic superhero should wear. Created by writer Harry Shorten and artist Irv Novick, he debuted in *Pep Comics* #1 (January 1940). An FBI man in everyday life this hero's avowed purpose was to "shield the U.S. government from all enemies." Minute-Man, also known as the "One Man Army," was first seen in *Master Comics* #11 (February 1941). He specialized in fighting assorted spies, saboteurs, and foreign invaders.

Captain America, the invention of Joe Simon and Jack Kirby, entered the field early in 1941. Unlike most superheroes up until then, Cap was given his own magazine from the start and didn't have try out anywhere else first. A Professor

Reinstein had invented a "strange seething liquid" and after getting an injection, Steve Rogers was transformed from a ninety-seven-pound weakling into a superhuman. After turning into Captain America, with suitable red, white, and blue costume, Rogers also joined the Army as a private. This made his double life somewhat difficult, but he managed to bring it off. He met Bucky Barnes in the service, an energetic, fearless lad described as "the mascot of the regiment." The two immediately teamed up against "vicious elements who seek to overthrow the U.S. government!"

Captain Battle was thought up by Jack Binder and first appeared in *Silver Streak* #10 (May 1941). This captain stood out from all the rest because he wore a black patch over his left eye. As his original story explained, he was a World War I veteran who was also a scientific genius, and he had "given his life to the scientific perfection of inventions which he uses to overcome evil and aggressive influences."

Marvel offered two more superpatriots in its *U.S.A. Comics*. They were the Defender and Mr. Liberty. Simon and Kirby did the cover for the magazine's first issue. Over at *Marvel Mystery Comics* a star-spangled hero named The Patriot set up his practice. Among the others from various houses were Captain Courageous, the Conqueror, Man of War, the Star-Spangled Kid, Super-American, Captain Freedom, Captain Flag, the Flag, Flagman, Major Victory, the Fighting Yank, Stormy Foster—the Great Defender, Yankee Doodle Jones, and U.S. Jones.

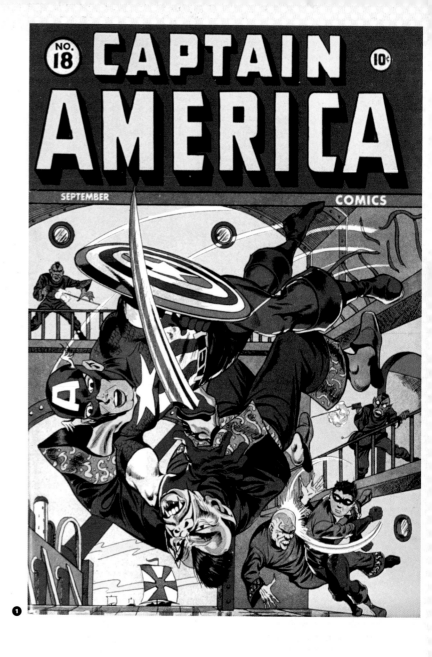

❶

❷

❶ ‥
CAPTAIN AMERICA #18
September 1942
Syd Shores
Captain America and Bucky alternated between battling German and Japanese opponents.

❷ ‥
MASTER COMICS #16
July 1941
Charles Sultan
Minute-Man seems to have wandered into the First World War by mistake.

WONDERWORLD COMICS #32
December 1941
Pierce Rice and Arturo Cazeneuve
Something old, something new, something borrowed, something red, white, and blue. Publisher Victor Fox found inspiration everywhere, especially in successful characters like the Shield and Captain America. Here he offers the public U.S. Jones.

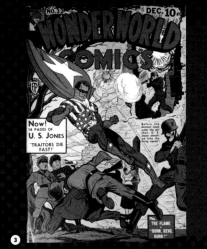

PEP COMICS #20
October 1941
Irv Novick
A poster-like cover with the Shield, Dusty, and the Hangman going to the aid of Nazi victims.

YANKEE COMICS #3
January 1942
Charles Sultan
Even though they had similar tastes in costumes, Yankee Doodle Jones and U.S. Jones apparently were not related.

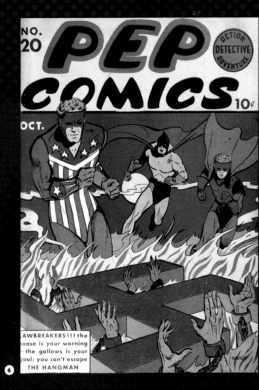

❹ ••

MAN OF WAR #1
November 1941
Paul Gustavson
According to the origin story, Man of War was created by Mars, the God of War.

❺ ••

DYNAMIC COMICS #1
October 1941
Charles Sultan
Major Victory defends his country from unspecified fascists, undaunted by the fact that his name is a pun.

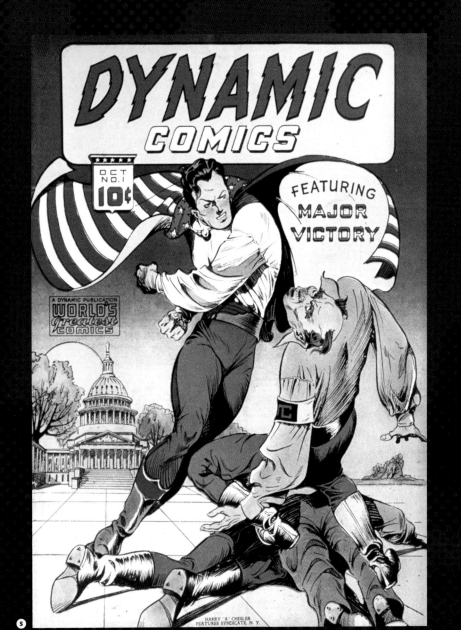

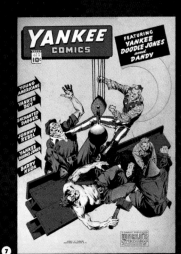

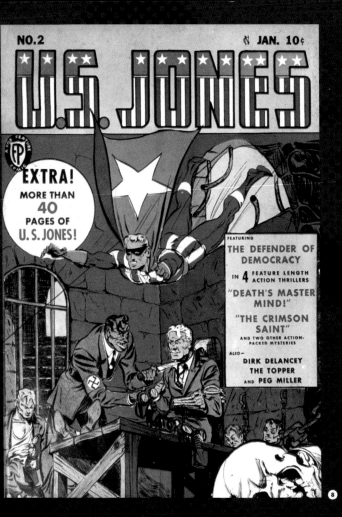

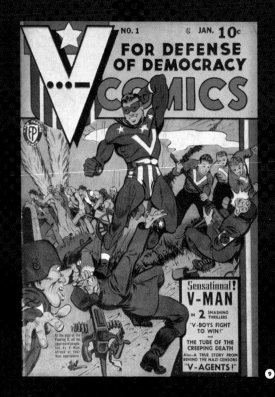

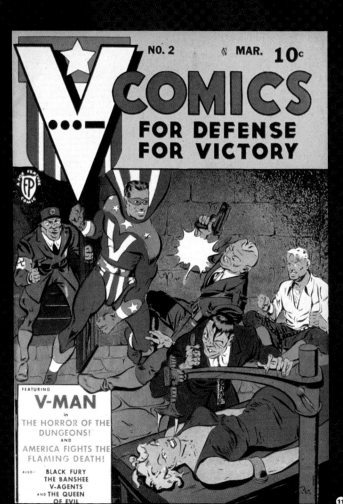

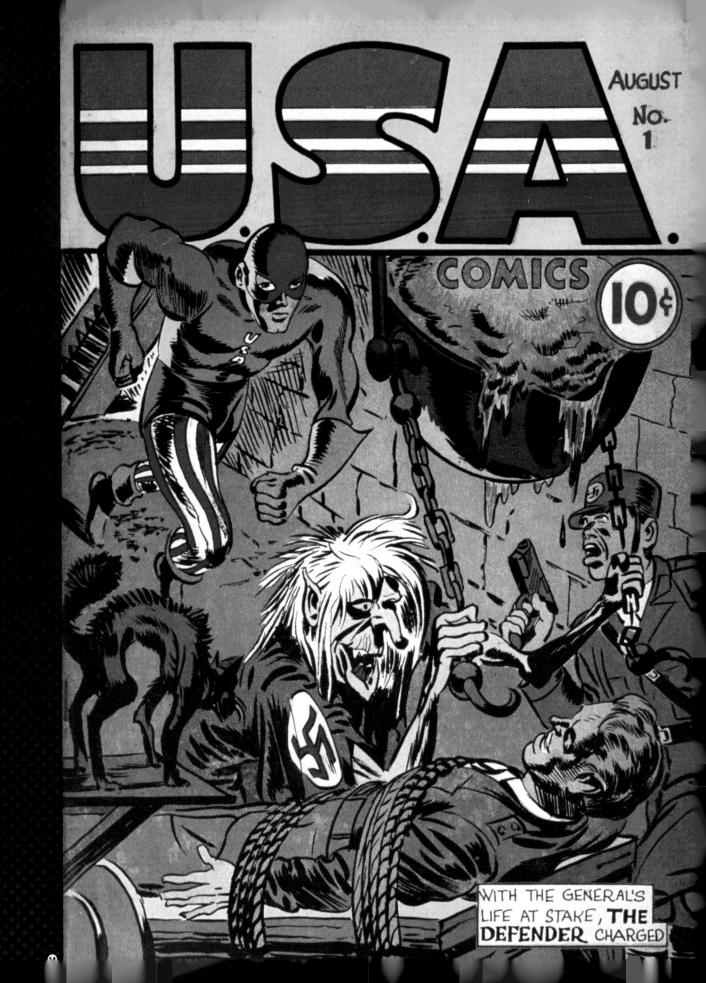

16 ••
CAPTAIN COURAGEOUS COMICS #6
March 1942
David Berg
Banner changed its name
with this issue and then was
seen no more. The captain
survived in *4 Favorites*.

17 ••
CAPTAIN BATTLE #5
Summer 1943
Al Gabrielle
A new cover for a reprint
of the first issue. Working for
Joe Simon and Jack Kirby
had a profound, if temporary,
effect on Gabrielle's style.

U.S. Jones first appeared in Fox' *Wonderworld* and
started a club for readers at once. Much like the club
Captain America was running, it was called the U.S.
Jones Cadets and cost ten cents to join. What kids got
for one thin dime was a National Emergency Kit,
"consisting of a membership card, a book of instruc-
tions on how to organize an AIR RAID COURIER
SERVICE, a secret code book, and a membership
badge." The coupon you were required to fill out and
sign included a loyalty oath that read, "I pledge
myself to defend my country, to maintain a constant
lookout for fifth columnists, and to carry out loyally
the duties assigned to me in time of national emergency." This was in the summer of 1941, several
months before America entered World War II.

15 ••
BANNER COMICS #3
September 1941
Jim Mooney
This is the first issue, and it
introduced Captain Courageous.

Several women were transformed into superpatriots during those same prewar months. A lady named USA the Spirit of Old Glory commenced her brief career in *Feature Comics* (March 1941). Miss America started in *Military Comics* #1 (August 1941), and a Miss Victory was first seen in *Captain Fearless* (August 1941). Over at Lev Gleason's, Pat Patriot was working in an aircraft factory when, suspecting her bosses of sabotage, she donned a red-white-and blue costume to become "America's Joan of Arc." She appeared in *Daredevil Comics* from #2 (August 1941) through #11 (June 1942). The talented Reed Crandall was one of several artists who illustrated her patriotic adventures. DC added Liberty Belle, a blonde heroine with a Veronica Lake hairdo, to its *Star-Spangled Comics* in 1943 after a tryout run in *Boy Commandos* the year before. Marvel added a Miss America of their own to *Marvel Mystery* in 1943. They gave her her own magazine the following year, but with its second issue it became a girls' publication with articles, fashion tips, etc.

❶❾

⓮ ••

FIGHT COMICS #17

February 1942

Dan Zolnerowich

This isn't a bad name
for a super-American either.
"How about we call him
Super-American?" And it
also sounds sort of like both
Superman and Captain America.
Quite probably Jerry Iger,
who ran Victor Fox a close second
when it came to brainstorms,
had a hand in this one.

⓮

⓳ ••

ALL-NEW COMICS #10

September 1944

Alex Schomburg

Captain Red Blazer, Sparky,
and the Boy Heroes put a stop
to a Japanese poison gas plot.
Any relation to Captain America,
Bucky, and the Young Allies
(or the Boy Commandos)
is purely coincidental.

A Brief History of Good Girl Art

The term "Good Girl Art" didn't come into use among comic book collectors, readers, and dealers until a few dozen years ago, but the phenomenon existed almost from the beginning of the funny-book business in the 1930s. Keep in mind that the term refers not to magazines that contained drawings of good girls but rather to those featuring good drawings of pretty young women. These pretty young women were most often scantily or provocatively clad.

The customers for such early titles as *Famous Funnies*, *Popular Comics*, and *Super Comics* were presumed to be children and the magazines were packaged and promoted accordingly. On the first two years of *Famous* covers, for example, you'll find only four young women depicted and all of them sedately presented. On its first two dozen covers, *Popular* showed just one full-grown woman, although Little Orphan Annie did pop up thirteen times. *Super*'s only young woman during its first two years was Winnie Winkle from the comic strips and she appeared on just three of the twenty-four covers.

Only one young woman is seen on the first two dozen covers of Major Nicholson's pioneering original material *New Fun*. She may, however, be the very first pretty girl in jeopardy ever depicted on the front of a comic book. The economical Major recycled an interior page of Clemens Gretter's *Don Drake on the*

Planet Saro for the third issue, and readers were thus provided with several panels showing Don's blonde ladyfriend being menaced by tentacled aliens. Major Nicholson's *New Comics* (later *New Adventure* and finally just plain *Adventure Comics*) didn't feature any women on its first twenty-four covers.

By the late 1930s, some of the publishers who were entering the field came to realize that a large portion of the audience for this upstart newsstand product was made up of adolescent boys or boys on the brink of adolescence. This inspired them and their editors in different ways. The more sedate, such as Detective Comics, Inc. (successor to Major Nicholson's outfit), added more adolescent boy characters, and this resulted in the advent of Robin the Boy Wonder and dozens of similarly inclined lads. *Detective Comics*, by the way, never showed a woman on its cover during

its early years. In fact, there was only one women in evidence on the first 100 covers. Even Batman's favorite opponent, the Cat Woman, was not seen out front until #122 (April 1947). Other publishers, most notably Fiction House, chose to feature sparsely clad young women on the front of their comic books early on. Confident that pubescent boys were interested in looking at such objects, they also made certain that there were plentiful supplies of provocative women inside their magazines as well.

One of the founding fathers of Good Girl Art was Samuel Maxwell Iger, better known as Jerry Iger. A onetime newspaper cartoonist possessed of a very primitive big-foot style, Iger was a dedicated entrepreneur. In 1937, after editing a short-lived comic book titled *Wow*, he intuited that there was going to be a comic book industry and that publishers, many of them moving into the field from the pulps or from girlie magazines, were going to be needing material. Iger started a shop to provide that material and was fortunate in getting one of his *Wow* contributors to team up with him. Talented and inventive as both an artist and a writer, Will Eisner was just twenty when he entered into an uneasy partnership with Iger. The earliest and most influential product of the new Eisner-Iger shop was *Jumbo Comics*, the magazine that introduced Sheena the Queen of the Jungle to America.

The blonde female Tarzan had originally appeared in an overseas tabloid called *Wags*, packaged by the shop. In 1938, Iger persuaded T.T. Scott, publisher of the Fiction House line of pulp-fiction magazines—

❶ ∙∙
GREEN MASK #8
December 1941
Louis Cazeneuve

② ··
MYSTERY MEN #4
November 1939
Lou Fine

③ ··
WEIRD COMICS #1
April 1940
George Tuska
Some early examples of
women as victims.

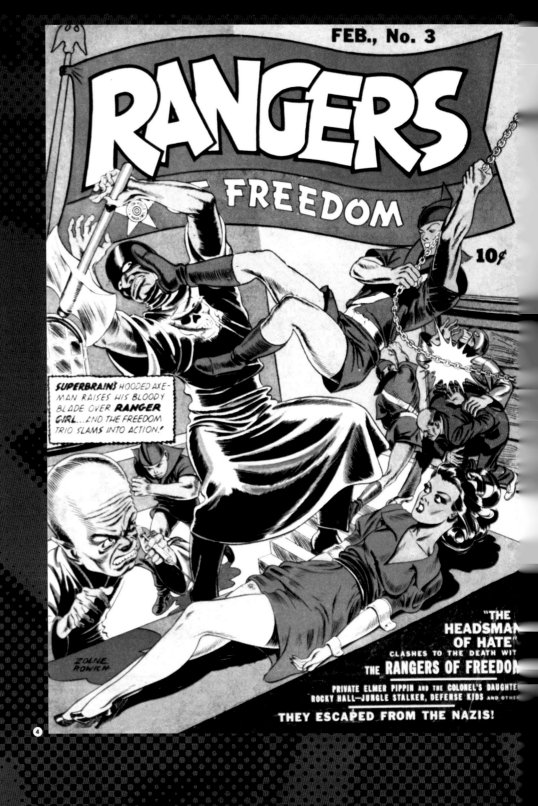

④ ··
RANGERS #3
February 1942
Dan Zolnerowich

Wings, *Jungle Stories*, *Fight Stories*, etc.—to go into the comic book trade. Their first venture was *Jumbo Comics*, a tabloid-sized funny book that recycled the old *Wags* material. The initial issues used the original printing plates, and instead of full-color, *Jumbo* simply used different colored paper for its jumbo pages. Initially, Sheena was not the leading lady, but by the second year, after the magazine had wisely shrunk to standard size and she had adopted her leopard-skin costume, she was the leading lady. From the eighteenth issue (August 1940) onward, she appeared on every cover.

The writing credit always went to W. Morgan Thomas, a dashing penname coined by Eisner. The original artist was Mort Meskin, and he was followed by Bob Powell, Robert Webb, and various volunteers from the bullpen. Eisner was the first to draw the jungle queen on a *Jumbo* cover. He was succeeded by Powell, Dan Zolnerowich, Artie Saaf, and others. Sheena's adventures were pretty much standard jungle-story fare, involving her with rampaging savages, evil slave traders, vicious ivory hunters, and, after World War II commenced, Nazi invaders. What distinguished her from Tarzan, Ka-Zar, and most of the other jungle comic book characters was the fact that she was quite a bit more interesting to look at. Her core audience of adolescent boys swelled appreciably during the War, when thousands of pin-up-happy GIs joined the *Jumbo* readership.

Eisner and Iger continued to put together magazines. For Fiction House, they also came up with *Jungle Comics*, *Planet Comics*, and *Wings Comics*. For the

❼ ·
JUNGLE COMICS #89
May 1947
Joe Doolin
Another villainous woman.

❽ ·
JUNGLE COMICS #46
October 1943
Rafael Astarita

more sedate Quality line, it was *Hit Comics*, *Crack Comics*, *National Comics*, etc. In 1940, Eisner left the shop to establish a studio of his own and turn out, among other features, *The Spirit*. Iger continued alone and from that point the product of the shop grew considerably broader, and the Good Girl Art-style burgeoned.

Late in 1939, Fiction House added *Jungle Comics* to its roster. The star of this new title was Kaanga, a blonde Tarzan impersonator. His mate, who shared most of his woodland adventures, was a dark-haired young lady named Ann. She wore a two-piece leopard-skin outfit, and the majority of other females seen in this particular stretch of jungle weren't noted for overdressing. On the covers Ann was sometimes seen in the role of rescue victim, but sometimes she actually took part in battles and skirmishes with the various threats that came to their wilderness turf. The scripts for the stories were credited to the alias Frank Riddell, and the artists included George Tuska, Dan Zolnerowich, John Celardo, Reed Crandell, Reuben Moreira, and Maurice Whitman. Two of them, Moreira and Celardo eventually went on to draw the *Tarzan* newspaper strip.

Jungle was also the home of Camilla, who, after a few false starts, developed into a successful Sheena surrogate. Also a blonde and billed as the Queen of the Jungle Empire, she wore a zebra-skin outfit rather than the traditional leopard-spotted togs. Most of the other features in the magazine—*Tabu-Wizard of the Jungle*, *Fantomah*, and *Wambi the Jungle Boy*—also managed to included young women with a minimum of clothing.

Fiction House's *Planet Comics* was the first comic book devoted exclusively to science fiction. All but three of its covers during its seventy-three issue run featured attractive young women not overly burdened by clothes. Since the youths who plunked down their dimes for *Planet Comics* were sci-fi fans as well, the covers also pictured bug-eyed alien creatures, stalwart spacemen blasting away with ray guns, and an abundance of rocket ships and futuristic locales.

As the 1940s progressed, the art and editorial contents of *Planet* placed increasing emphasis on the female form, and new lady stars were added. Mysta of the Moon, also known as a "queen of science," made her debut in issue #36 and Futura followed in #43. *The Lost World* began in the November 1942 issue and dealt with a future Earth after it had been brutally invaded by the "slaughter-mad warriors of Volta." These unhandsome green Voltans were unashamedly nasty and behaved in an even worse fashion than the Nazis they obviously were based on. Though the hero of the feature was a husky chap named Hunt Bowman, most eyes were on his female companion, a nearly naked blonde named Lyssa.

The major cover artist was pulp veteran Joe Doolin, who drew over three dozen of the Planet Comics covers. Dan Zolnerowich was the second most prolific cover artist, drawing all but one of the covers from January of 1941 through July of 1943. *Planet* continued until the winter of 1953, a citadel of Good Girl Art until the end.

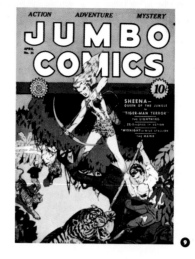

9 ··
JUMBO COMICS #26
April 1941
Nick Cardy
Sheena was the first woman to appear regularly on comic book covers in heroic roles.

10 ·
JUMBO COMICS #55
September 1943
Artie Saaf

PLANET COMICS #28

January 1944

Joe Doolin

The covers always more
than lived up to *Planet*'s
slogan—"Weird Adventures
on Other Worlds."

14 ..

PLANET COMICS #31

July 1944

Joe Doolin

Something new in the way
of a religious experience.

15 ..

PLANET COMICS #24

May 1943

Dan Zolnerowich

For a switch,
a woman rescues a guy.

Launched at the same time as its SF sister, *Fight Comics* originally devoted itself to action and adventure yarns, with an occasional prize-fight story tossed in. The magazine introduced a low-key superhero known as Power Man in the third issue and a Captain America surrogate, called Super-American, in the fifteenth (October 1941). Toward the end of that year, women began to figure prominently on the covers. In 1942, after America officially entered the War, they were often seen, with skirts hiked, being threatened or tortured by Japanese soldiers. Zolnerowich and Doolin provided many of the covers here, too.

Fight Comics #32 (June 1944) introduced Tiger Girl, another Sheena simulacrum, who wore a two-piece tiger-skin bathing suit. Also known as Princess Vishnu, she resided in a hidden temple and looked after the people and animals in her part of India. The artist was Matt Baker, who would become one of the most successful and prolific practitioners of Good Girl Art in the years immediately after the end of the World War II.

Wings Comics, its name inspired by that of Fiction House's successful aviation pulp, first appeared on the stands in the autumn of 1940. The earliest comic book devoted exclusively to flying, it initially concentrated on fully-clothed air heroes. Its lone feature starring a female—*Jane Martin, War Nurse*—was quite sedate in its earliest months. Among the other characters in the early years were Clipper Kirk, the Skull Squad, Greasemonkey Griffin, and Captain Wings. The stories offered airborne thrills and on-the-ground

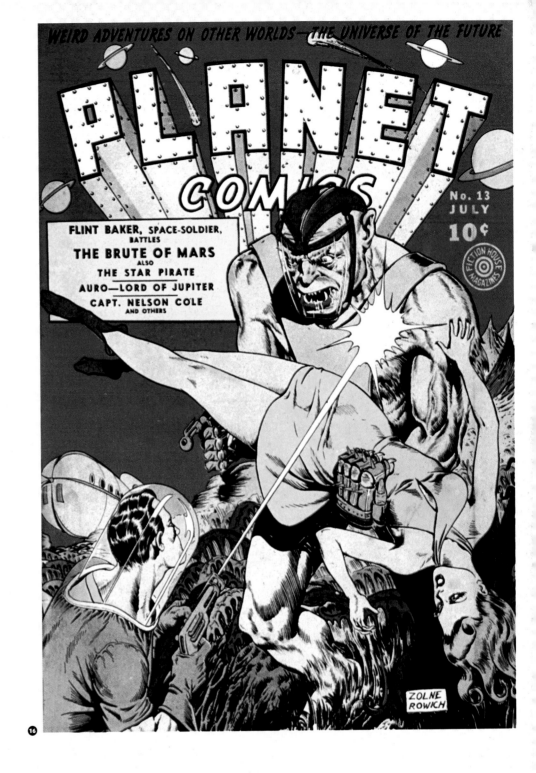

16 ••
PLANET COMICS #13
July 1941
Dan Zolnerowich
All the classic ingredients—
hero with a ray gun, tinted
alien, sparsely clad girl in
danger and, in the background,
a rocket ship.

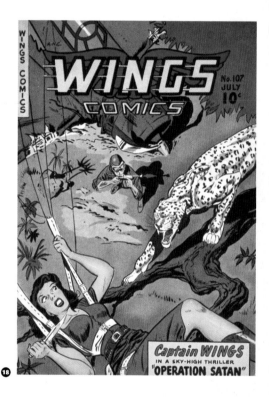

⓱ •

WINGS COMICS #75
July 1949
Bob Lubbers
Lubbers was an expert at drawing both airplanes and pretty women.

⓲ •

WINGS COMICS #107
July 1949
Bob Lubbers

19 •

FIGHT COMICS #24

February 1943

Dan Zolnerowich

A war nurse as victim.

20 •

FIGHT COMICS #38

June 1945

Joe Doolin

Another women to be rescued, another cover that has nothing to do with anything to be found inside.

19

intrigue in varied locations such as Egypt, England, the Balkans, China, Malaya, and Libya. The covers concentrated on airplanes.

At the beginning of 1942, when the post exchange was becoming as important an outlet as the newsstand, *Wings* turned more attention to the female form. By the war years, with Iger in charge of producing the art, several artists who could draw not only airplanes but pretty women were added to the crew, among them Bob Lubbers, Artie Saaf, and Nick Cardy. Raised skirts and cleavage were as frequently seen as propellers and machine guns. Ladies started playing an important role in just about every story. Jane Martin took to showing up for work in provocative attire and, on occasion, in her undies.

20

21 •

FIGHT COMICS #49

April 1947

Joe Doolin

Tiger Girl was one of many postwar jungle queens. Notice that, true to her name, her costume is made of tiger skin. Her tiger friends didn't seem to frown on this.

21

The postwar years found *Wings* in an especially girl-crazy mood. Every monthly cover from the spring of 1947 to the fall of 1949 showed a pretty and usually scantily clad young woman. There was also, to be sure, at least one airplane on every cover. The reliable Bob Lubbers drew all twenty-eight of these catchy covers.

Fiction House brought forth *Rangers Comics* next. By #3, women with hiked skirts were a prominent part of each cover layout. Zolnerowich and Artie Saaf took turns with the early covers. The eventual star of the magazine made her debut in #21 (February 1945). Billed as a "Frontier Queen" and the "Flame Girl of the Wild West," Firehair was a redheaded heroine who operated in a sort of Hollywood version of the Old West. Like many another character in Western novels and cowboy movies, Firehair had been raised by Indians after the death of her parents. Adopted by the Dakota tribe that took her in, she remained with them after reaching maturity. Clad in a skimpy buckskin dress, she acted as a champion of her people and helped them battle against the continuous stream of predatory white men who sought to murder, cheat, rob, and take advantage of them. True to their pulp background, Fiction House stuck flamboyant pulpwood titles on the Girl of the Golden West's adventures, and covers touted epics such as *The Outlaw Pack of Hangman's Mesa* and *Brides of the Buffalo Men*. Lee Elias, later to draw the Black Cat's adventures, was the initial artist. When he moved on, Lubbers took over.

Another sort of female character was also emerging in comic books at the same time as the Good Girl Art icons. She was more a Do-Good Girl, be she policewoman, masked avenger, or superhuman. The point was, she usually relied on her capabilities rather than on just her sexual attractiveness. And, in most cases, she rarely appeared on a cover. The exception was Wonder Woman, who was highly visible on every cover of DC's *Sensation Comics* from #1 (January 1942) through #106 (November-December 1951). She obviously also dominated the covers of her own *Wonder Woman* magazine, begun in 1942, for many years and could also be spotted sharing covers of *All Star* and *Comic Cavalcade* now and then.

Wonder Woman's only serious competitor in the cover girl field was Mary Marvel. Captain Marvel's teenage sister appeared on fifty covers of *Wow Comics*, from 1943 to 1947. She was also on more than two dozen on her own *Mary Marvel* magazine, and she shared all eighty-nine covers of *The Marvel Family* with her male kin.

22 ••
SEVEN SEAS COMICS #3
August 1946
Matt Baker
The lady in the abbreviated sarong was known as South Sea Girl.

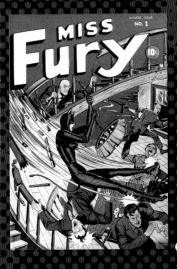

23

24

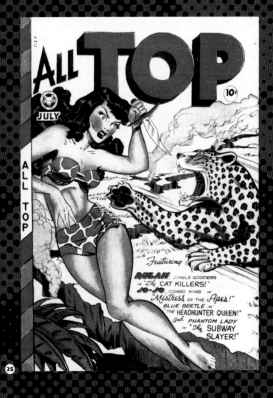

25

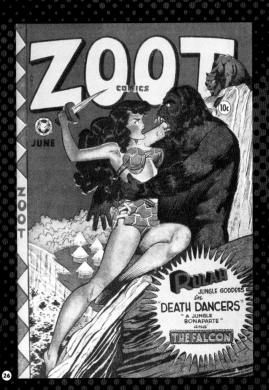

26

27

23 ••

MISS FURY #1

Winter 1942

Al Plastino

Reprints of Tarpé Mills'
Sunday page, bringing even
more bondage and fetishism
to comic books.

24 ••

PHANTOM LADY #17

April 1948

Matt Baker

Phantom Lady had matured
somewhat since her debut in
Police Comics back in 1941.

25 ••

ALL TOP #12

July 1948

The Iger Shop

Who better to provide
Fox with jungle girl clones than
Jerry Iger, who'd had a hand
in the creation of Sheena?
Rulah starred in several titles.

26 ••

ZOOT #15

June 1948

The Iger Shop

27 ••

RULAH #17

August 1948

The Iger Shop

Featuring **THE BLACK TERROR**, *Nemesis of Crime*

ANC

EXCITING COMICS

10¢

MAR. No. 66

in THIS issue

JUDY of the **JUNGLE** Queen of the Danger Lands

ROGER DODGER Tops in Teen-Age Fun

RICK HOWARD Gun-Slinging Cowboy

And Other Features!

28

10¢

THRILLING COMICS

Featuring THE EXCITING ADVENTURES OF *PRINCESS PANTHA*

29

Lesser known ladies such as Wildfire, Liberty Belle, Betty Bates, and The Spider Widow remained hidden inside the pages of their respective comic books.

After the World War II ended and in the middle and late 1940s, the attitudes of many publishers changed, and more and more women were seen on covers. They were, however, mostly of the Good Girl Art school. The Pines-Margulies line made a conspicuous change in many of their titles. At *Thrilling Comics*, Doc Strange was discarded as a cover icon and replaced by a sexy jungle girl named Princess Pantha. *Exciting Comics* ignored the Black Terror in favor of first a costumed female crime fighter known as Miss Masque and then a redheaded jungle girl called Judy of the Jungle. At *Startling Comics* and *Wonder Comics*, it was sparsely clad sci-fi heroines on the covers.

Victor Fox returned aggressively to comic books in the middle 1940s and, with the help of Jerry Iger's shop, revived Phantom Lady and endowed her with a title of her own. The artist was Matt Baker, one of the masters of Good Girl Art, and his version of the revived character looked quite a bit like popular cheesecake model Bettie Page. Fox also introduced jungle-girl characters, notably Rulah, who had her own magazine and also was featured in *Zoot Comics*. For good measure, she and Phantom Lady both appeared in *All Top Comics*. Fox and Iger also produced *Zegra, Jungle Empress*. Over at Robert Farrell's Ajax-Farrell Publications the jungle-empress comic book was *Vooda*, and at L.B. Cole's *Terrors of the Jungle* one found the likes of Tangi.

30 ••

WONDER COMICS #17
April 1948
Alex Schomburg
Tara, a space pirate,
became the leading lady during
Wonder's final year.

31 ••

STARTLING COMICS #49
January 1947
Alex Schomburg
If you look carefully, you'll spot
Lance Lewis, Space Detective
in the background.

32 ··

THRILLING TRUE CRIME CASES #49
July 1952
L.B. Cole

33 ··

CRIME DOES NOT PAY #22
July 1942 (the first issue)
Charles Biro
The first of the genre that
would eventually help the
comic book industry survive
in the postwar years. And
then lead to its near downfall.

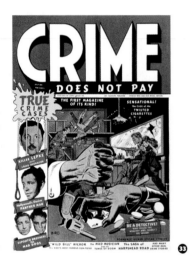

33

35

36

34 ··

ELLERY QUEEN #2
Summer 1952
Jack Kamen
Not quite the cerebral EQ
of books, magazines, radio,
and movies.

32

34

35 ··

TRUE CRIME
Middle 1940s
Charles Biro
A typical Biro cover,
this one for a reprint of
two issues of *CDNP*.

36 ·

CRIME AND PUNISHMENT #1
July 1948
Charles Biro
A wordy cover that still manages
to get in some Good Girl Art
images. Publisher Lev Gleason
didn't get around to imitating
his *Crime Does Not Pay* until
dozens of other publications
had already done it.

The true-crime comic book had gotten started in 1942 when publisher Lev Gleason converted *Silver Streak Comics* into *Crime Does Not Pay* and gave Charles Biro and Bob Wood the job of editing it. For a few years CDNP had little or no competition. After World War II, rival companies, finding that superheroes weren't selling very well, took note of the impressive sales figures that Gleason's magazine was showing. Many of them turned to crime. Over the next few years, scores of crime comics hit the stands, most of them with attractive young women somewhere on the

covers. The titles included *Crime Exposed*, *Fight Against Crime*, *Gangsters and Gunmolls*, *Crime Must Pay the Penalty*, *Justice Traps the Guilty*, *Real Clue Crime Stories*, *Crimes by Women*, *Famous Crimes*, *Crime Detective*, *Wanted*, *Authentic Police Cases*, *March of Crime*, *Crime SuspenStories*, and *True Crime*.

Romance titles, of which there were hundreds, also proved to sell well. Horror titles had impressive sales, too. By the beginning of the 1950s, comic books were much different than they'd been a decade earlier. There had been criticism of comics from their earliest days, but it increased now that sex and violence had replaced superheroes and funny animals. Eventually there were protests, investigations, and the collapse of much of the industry. The new competition from television didn't help either.

But that's another story.

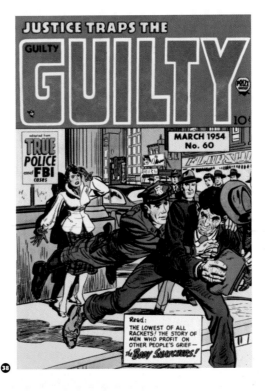

37 •
CLUE COMICS #11
December 1946
Fred Kida
Clue was already in transition by this time and would soon change into a true-crime comic titled *Real Clue*.

38 •
JUSTICE TRAPS THE GUILTY #60
March 1954
Marv Stein
One of the scores of crime comics on the stands in the early 1950s.

The Stuff at the Back of the Book
Collecting Comic Books

I f browsing through this compilation of comic book covers from the 1930s and 1940s has inspired you to consider collecting Golden Age magazines think twice. Fine, or even good, copies of books from this period are very rare and very expensive. For instance, a copy of the *Action Comics* #7 shown in these pages would cost you between $1,300 and $13,000, depending on the condition. The *More Fun Comics* we illustrated is priced anywhere from $820 to $8,400, and a fine copy of *Daredevil Battles Hitler* would run about $5,000 (and a near mint copy at almost twice that). If you simply want to enjoy old covers, our book is a much more economical solution.

If your curiosity is aroused, however, you might want to pick up a copy of *The Overstreet Comic Book Price Guide*. A new edition comes out every year, and it'll tell you what just about every comic book published between 1900 and 2000 is worth. Almost any comic shop, and many bookstores, can sell you the latest edition.

Several publishers including Marvel and DC have re-issue programs and reprint Golden Age material in both hardcover collections and comic book formats. Most comic book shops stock a lot of this material, and *Comics Buyer's Guide*, a weekly tabloid, offers news about them and a variety of other comics, old and new. *CBG* also lists just about every local comic book convention taking place around the country. Conventions are another good place to track down Golden Age material.

A Concise Bibliography

Gerber, Ernst and Mary. *The Photo-Journal Guide to Comic Books*. Vols 1 and 2. Minden: Gerber Publishing Co., 1989.

Goulart, Ron. *Great History of Comic Books*. Chicago, IL: Contemporary Books, 1986.

—, *Over 50 Years of American Comic Books*. Lincolnwood: Publications International, Ltd., 1991.

—, *The Great Comic Book Artists*. Vol 1. New York, NY: St. Martin's Press, 1986.

—, *The Comic Book Reader's Companion*. New York, NY: HarperPerennial, 1993.

Harvey, Robert C. *The Art of the Comic Book*. Jackson, MS: University Press of Mississippi, 1996.

Keltner, Howard. *Golden Age Comic Books Index*. Gainesville, TX: Keltner, 1998.

Lupoff, Dick and Don Thompson. *All In Color For A Dime*. Iola, IL: Krause Publications, 1997.

Simon, Joe. *The Comic Book Makers*. New York, NY: Crestwood /11, 1990.

Bullet Values

- $5 to $100
- • $101 to $1000
- • • $1001 to $10,000
- • • • $10,001 to $20,000
- • • • • $20,001 and beyond

Copyright Credits

FAMOUS FUNNIES ················ 4

Barney Google © 1923 Cupples and Leon Company

The Funnies © 1930 Dell Publishing Co.

Funnies on Parade, Famous Funnies, Famous Comics © 1933, 1934, 1935, 1936, 1937, 1941, 1953, 1954 Eastern Color Printing Co.

JUMPING ON THE BANDWAGON ·········· 15

The Funnies, Popular Comics © 1937, 1938, 1940, 1941 Dell Publishing Co.

Crackajack Funnies, Super Comics © 1940, 1941 Whitman Publishing Co., Inc.

Feature Funnies © 1938 Quality Comics Group

Future Comics © 1940 David McKay Publishers

Big Shot Comics © 1940 Columbia Comics Corp.

MAJOR NICHOLSON ENTERS THE FRAY ······· 25

All cover images in this chapter © DC Comics, Inc.

BRAND NEW AND ORIGINAL ·············· 32

The Comics Magazine © 1936 Comics Magazine Co.

Funny Pages, Funny Picture Stories, Detective Picture Stories, Keen Detective Funnies, Western Picture Stories, Star Comics, Star Ranger © 1936, 1937, 1938, 1939, 1940 Centaur Publications, Inc.

THIS MEANS WAR

THE SUPERPATRIOTS

A BRIEF HISTORY OF GOOD GIRL ART

COMICLAND
1948
Just think if this
boy owned 'em all today.